DELVING DEEP

RESEARCH METHODOLOGY IN STRATEGY AND MANAGEMENT

Series Editors: Paula O'Kane, Aaron F. McKenny, Sotirios Paroutis, and John R. Busenbark

PREVIOUSLY PUBLISHED VOLUMES

RESEARCH METHODOLOGY IN STRATEGY AND
MANAGEMENT, VOLUME 15

DELVING DEEP: TECHNIQUES WE WISHED WE HAD KNOWN AS EMERGING SCHOLARS

EDITED BY

PAULA O'KANE
University of Otago, New Zealand

JOHN R. BUSENBARK
University of Notre Dame, USA

AARON F. MCKENNY
Indiana University Bloomington, USA

AND

SOTIRIOS PAROUTIS
University of Warwick, UK

United Kingdom – North America – Japan
India – Malaysia – China

Emerald Publishing Limited
Emerald Publishing, Floor 5, Northspring, 21-23 Wellington Street, Leeds LS1 4DL

First edition 2025

Reprints and permissions service
Contact: www.copyright.com

British Library Cataloguing in Publication Data
A catalogue record for this book is available from the British Library

ISBN: 978-1-83797-027-8 (Print)
ISBN: 978-1-83797-026-1 (Online)
ISBN: 978-1-83797-028-5 (Epub)

ISSN: 1479-8387 (Series)

INVESTOR IN PEOPLE

CONTENTS

ABOUT THE EDITORS

Paula O'Kane is a Senior Lecturer in Human Resource Management at the University of Otago, Dunedin (New Zealand). She has expertise in interpretative qualitative research across a range of areas including performance management, social media, and the future of work. She has extensive expertise in Computer Aided Qualitative Data Analysis and has published in *Research Methodology in Strategy and Management*, as well as *Organizational Research Methods, Human Resource Management Journal, Studies in Higher Education*, among others.

John R. Busenbark is the Mary Jo and Richard M. Kovacevich Associate Professor of Management and Organization in the Mendoza College of Business at the University of Notre Dame, Indiana, USA.

Aaron F. McKenny is an Assistant Professor of Management and Entrepreneurship at the Kelley School of Business, Indiana University, and was the recipient of the 2020 *Sage Publications/RMD Lawrence R. James Early Career Award* from the Academy of Management Research Methods Division. His methods research emphasizes the dissemination and advancement of content analysis in organizational research and has been published in journals such as *Organizational Research Methods, Journal of Applied Psychology, Journal of Management, Annual Review of Organizational Psychology and Organizational Behavior, Research Methods in Strategy and Management*, and *Family Business Review*. He is a coeditor of the *Research Methodology in Strategy and Management* series and sits on the review boards of *Academy of Management Review, Organizational Research Methods, Journal of Management, Journal of Business Venturing, Entrepreneurship Theory and Practice*, and *Family Business Review*.

Sotirios Paroutis is a Professor of Strategic Management at the Warwick Business School (United Kingdom). He primarily uses qualitative methods to study the practices and processes organizational actors employ when dealing with strategic tensions. His work has been published in *Research Methodology in Strategy and Management, Strategic Management Journal, Organization Studies*, and *Long Range Planning*, among others.

ABOUT THE CONTRIBUTORS

Andrew B. Blake is an Assistant Professor of Management in the Rawls College of Business at Texas Tech University. He received his PhD from the University of Arkansas. Andrew's research broadly focuses on the intersection of social psychology and the micro-foundations of strategy, emphasizing attention on the impact that CEOs and entrepreneurs have on organizational outcomes.

Steven Boivie is the Carroll & Dorothy Conn Chair in New Ventures Leadership at the Mays Business School at Texas A&M University. He received his PhD in Strategic Management from the University of Texas at Austin, his Master's degree from Brigham Young University, and his Bachelor's degree from Utah State University. He is primarily interested in how behavioral and social forces affect human actors at the top of the organization, and he conducts research in the areas of corporate governance, top executives, and directors. His research has been published in the *Academy of Management Journal*, *Strategic Management Journal*, *Organization Science*, *Journal of Applied Psychology*, *Academy of Management Annals*, and *Journal of Management*. Steve's research has also been mentioned in a number of press outlets including the *Wall Street Journal*, *Harvard Business Review* online, Forbes.com, *IR Magazine*, *Bloomberg*, *The Economist*, and more.

Joseph S. Harrison is an Associate Professor of Strategy in the Haslam College of Business at the University of Tennessee. He received his PhD in Strategic Management from Texas A&M University. His research focuses on social and behavioral aspects of strategic leaders and using content analytic techniques to understand organizational phenomena. Through his research, he has codeveloped multiple machine learning applications to extract meaning from unstructured text and provide insights into executive personality, corporate governance, risk, and performance. His work has been published in *Academy of Management Journal*, *Academy of Management Review*, *Journal of Management*, *Organization Science*, and *Strategic Management Journal*, among others. It has also been highlighted in press outlets like *Harvard Business Review* online, Fortune.com, and the TEK2Day podcast.

Aaron D. Hill is an Associate Professor in the Management Department of the Warrington College of Business at the University of Florida. He received his PhD at Oklahoma State University. His research focuses on strategic leadership and governance, examining the implications of executives for organizational outcomes.

Timothy D. Hubbard is an Assistant Professor of Management in the Mendoza College of Business, University of Notre Dame. He received his PhD from the University of Georgia. His research focuses on behavioral strategy – the cognitive and social factors that influence strategic decisions and their outcomes. He serves as a Director of the University of Notre Dame's Virtual Reality Laboratory. His research appears in the *Academy of Management Journal*, the *Strategic Management Journal*, the *Journal of Management*, the *Journal of Management Studies*, and the *Academy of Management Discoveries*, among others. He teaches strategic management and organizational theory.

Amrit Panda is a PhD student in the Management Department in the Rawls College of Business at Texas Tech University. He received his Master's in Human Resource Management from the Tata Institute of Social Sciences, India. His research interests lie broadly around upper echelons and competitive behavior of firms. Specifically, he is interested in exploring how CEOs and top management teams shape competitive strategy and its subsequent effect on firm performance and other strategic outcomes.

Oleg V. Petrenko is an Assistant Professor in the Strategy, Entrepreneurship, Venture, and Innovation Department at the Sam M. Walton College of Business at the University of Arkansas. He received his PhD from Oklahoma State University. His research broadly focuses on the micro-foundations of strategy in large corporations and new ventures. Specifically, he examines the psychology of executives and entrepreneurs and how it impacts strategic decision-making and firm performance. Oleg's research focuses on creating knowledge that will help the leaders of tomorrow be successful at leading their organizations and taking on new challenges.

Timothy J. Quigley is the Georgia Athletic Associate Professor of Management in the Terry College of Business at the University of Georgia. He received his PhD from Pennsylvania State University and is broadly interested in CEOs, CEO succession, and how CEOs impact organization outcomes. Tim is currently an Associate Editor at *Strategic Management Journal*.

Dean A. Shepherd, Bachelor of Applied Science (RMIT), MBA and PhD (Bond University, Australia), is the Ray and Milann Siegfried Professor of Entrepreneurship at the Mendoza College of Business, Notre Dame University. He has held positions at the Kelley School of Business, Indiana University, the Leeds School of Business, University of Colorado, and the Lally School of Management, Rensselaer Polytechnic Institute. His research and teaching are in the field of entrepreneurship; he investigates the decision-making involved in leveraging cognitive and other resources to act on opportunities, responding with resilience to adversity, learning from experimentation (including failure), and the dark side of entrepreneurship. He has authored over 20 books and 180 publications in top management and entrepreneurship journals with over 80,000 Google sites. Dean is a Fellow of the Academy of Management. From the Entrepreneurs Division of the Academy of Management, Dean has been awarded the "Dedication to

Entrepreneurship Award", the "Mentor Award", and the "Foundational Paper Award" (twice). He is the past Editor-in-Chief of the *Journal Business Venturing*. He is on the editorial boards of the *Academy of Management Journal*, the *Academy of Management Review*, *Entrepreneurship Theory and Practice*, *Strategic Entrepreneurship Journal*, and the *Journal of Management Studies*.

Eric W. K. Tsang is the Dallas World Salute Distinguished Professor at the Jindal School of Management, University of Texas at Dallas, and is a Fellow of the Academy of International Business. He received his PhD from the University of Cambridge. His main research interests include organizational learning, strategic alliances, corporate social responsibility, entrepreneurship, and philosophical analysis of methodological issues. He has published widely in leading business journals, such as *Academy of Management Journal*, *Academy of Management Review*, *Journal of International Business Studies*, *Marketing Science*, *MIS Quarterly*, and *Strategic Management Journal*, and is the author of the books *The Philosophy of Management Research* and *Explaining Management Phenomena: A Philosophical Treatise*. His publications have been well cited by fellow researchers. For example, his article "Social Capital, Networks, and Knowledge Transfer" (with Andrew Inkpen) is the winner of the 2015 Academy of Management Review Decade Award.

Michael Villano is a Research Assistant Professor of Psychology in the College of Arts and Letters at the University of Notre Dame.

BUILDING AN EMPIRICAL BODY OF EVIDENCE: DEVELOPING RAPPORT WITH REVIEWERS AND OVERCOMING SKEPTICISM IN STRATEGIC MANAGEMENT RESEARCH

Timothy J. Quigley

University of Georgia, USA

ABSTRACT

As the field of strategic management has evolved, expectations for the empirical evidence presented in manuscripts have risen substantially. Rather than a single model testing a hypothesis with a p-value below a standard threshold being sufficient, reviewers, editors, and eventual readers now demand additional evidence including multiple tests, advanced statistical models, alternative specifications, interpretation of practical rather than just statistical significance, and more. Reviewers appear to be increasingly skeptical and often raise a seemingly endless number of questions. In this chapter, I outline the idea of a body of evidence and suggest ways authors can build their evidence by anticipating reviewer questions and structuring manuscripts accordingly. Doing so allows authors to overcome skepticism by building positive rapport and trust with reviewers and the ultimate readers of their work. I conclude by discussing the review process where I offer suggestions about how reviewers and editors might adapt to this changing landscape. I specifically argue that all studies are flawed. Rather than asking for a single study to do more to address small inconsistencies or puzzling results, I suggest gatekeepers in the review process should consider the possibility that publishing and allowing research conversations to flourish might result in greater knowledge generation over time.

Delving Deep
Research Methodology in Strategy and Management, Volume 15, 1–22
Copyright © 2025 Timothy J. Quigley
Published under exclusive licence by Emerald Publishing Limited
ISSN: 1479-8387/doi:10.1108/S1479-838720240000015001

Keywords: Building a body of evidence; empirical research; trust; robustness; authoring; reviewing

INTRODUCTION

When you submit an empirical manuscript to a journal, you enter an asynchronous dialogue with a review team composed of an action editor and a set of anonymous reviewers. In doing so, you have two primary tasks. First, you must convince the review team that your ideas have merit. There is some debate about what this entails. The oft cited Davis treatise "That's Interesting" argues that papers should be interesting, novel, or counterintuitive and that they should create a "movement of the mind" by confronting taken-for-granted assumptions (Davis, 1971). Others stress the importance of addressing problems that are relevant to society while noting that an extreme focus on novelty might predispose our research toward chance findings and encourage troubling behavior like p-hacking and HARKING (hypothesizing after results are known) (Bettis et al., 2016; Tihanyi, 2020). As Bettis et al. note, it seems odd that the world would only be arranged so "that all phenomena of research importance are counterintuitive (p. 260)." Rather, they argue, we should "return the word interesting to its standard English language meaning of something that you want to learn more about (p. 260)." To this end, Huff (1999, p. 3) conveys the importance of positioning research within one or more ongoing scholarly "conversations," while Colquitt and George (2011) proffer that research should address big problems, change conversations, encourage new discussions, and provide insights for practice.

I'm of the opinion that generating interest is part of the creative process of research. It's hard to fully define, up front, all the ways something can be interesting, but we all know it when we see it. In a classic case of equifinality, there exist numerous creative ways to generate interest from readers (and, before that, reviewers) but, without it, your chances of success fade quickly as reviewers find conceptual cause to recommend rejection before even considering your empirical efforts. Nevertheless, this first imperative is conceptual in nature, focused mostly on the topic, framing, and motivation for a study.

Should you succeed in the first task of generating interest – a topic which receives ongoing attention from editors and seminal scholars alike – consideration moves to the second task. Here, your aim is to convince reviewers that your empirical results are robust, that they support your conceptual arguments and hypotheses, that the related inferences reasonably reflect what can be concluded from your data and analyses, and that these likely reflect the state of things in the population of interest. Frank (2000), the progenitor of the increasingly ubiquitous impact threshold of a confounding variable (ITCV) test, often refers to this as engaging in conversation with skeptics of empirical work. Frank surmises that it is incumbent on authors to assume readers are skeptical of the study's methodological procedures and to conduct (and explain) sufficient empirical techniques to assuage that trepidation.

The purpose of this chapter is to further address this second task, which has received far less attention than its initial counterpart. In doing so, I will offer the concept of *"building a body of evidence"* as your objective in this dialogue with methodological skeptics. No research project is perfect. No set of conclusions can be supported uniformly by every empirical test. Rather, your goal is to present a convincing body of evidence to persuade readers that your results are robust, and that you questioned your empirical inferences by subjecting supportive findings to the same scrutiny as you would if the results didn't work out. Doing this conveys your findings are trustworthy and likely reflective of something happening in the world. Here, the creative process continues, and the savvy scholar can use descriptive statistics, multiple tests, alternative specifications, and other means to craft a robust story that builds further interest in a paper through the strength and comprehensiveness of the empirical evidence. Done well, it creates a dialogue with reviewers and, once published, the readers as well.

Those who have been through the review process might quibble with the characterization of a paper submission as the "beginning of a dialogue." As the "gatekeepers of science" (Crane, 1967, p. 195), reviewers clearly have an active voice in the process. They are chosen from among a pool of experts in the field and, as Frank (2000) points out, they generally assume the role of a skeptic who must be convinced through a collection of persuasive evidence that the arguments merit publication and empirical findings are legitimate. Reviewers exercise a certain privilege where they get to tell authors what they like and what they don't like without ever having to directly face the author(s) they are assessing. Unless the manuscript is given a revise and resubmit, authors don't have much of a chance to engage in a "dialogue" by responding to criticism. If a paper is accepted, authors become known while reviewers enjoy anonymity. The potential problems within this process are well documented (Miller, 2006; Starbuck, 2003).

At first glance, I can see doubters of my view instinctively making the case that there's no "dialogue" in this process, but hear me out. My argument is that as reviewers digest a paper, they are stimulated by the writing to ask a series of seemingly rhetorical questions. While they turn the pages of your manuscript, reviewers repeatedly ask "but what about. . .," "why didn't you. . ..," "but did you consider. . .," or "what happens if . . .." I say "rhetorical" because, while reviewers (and later, readers) would like an answer, the authors are not physically present to offer one. Knowing that reviewers engage in such self-dialogue, an astute scholar can try to anticipate these questions and use them to assemble a set of logical arguments, alternative specifications, and supplemental analyses that effectively addresses those rhetorical questions *as the reviewer raises them silently in their own mind.* Done successfully, an author can have an asynchronous dialogue across time and space with reviewers. Yet, doing so requires that authors have some foresight created largely through a willingness to solicit critical feedback and be critical of one's own work.

To be clear, however, this chapter is not about simply piling up multiple statistical tests to overwhelm reviewers. They will see through that and doing so, at best, proves superfluous and cumbersome for all parties involved. Further, this is not about extensive use of jargon, technical terms, or seemingly advanced methodological wizardry to make a point. Of course, many papers call for complex statistical methods and they should be used (and clearly explained) when needed. However, their use can, at times, create more problems than they solve (Certo et al., 2016; Semadeni et al., 2014). Rather, building a body of evidence is about telling a story through descriptive statistics, formal empirical tests, alternative specifications, supplemental tests, and examples that flow logically from your conceptual arguments.

These ideas were primarily developed through my own journey trying to publish my research, sparring with reviewers (who are, more often than not, correct), through work as an associate editor, and by collaborating with and teaching applied econometrics to doctoral students. In developing these ideas, some colleagues insisted much of it should already be well understood by most strategic management scholars. Perhaps that's true. On the other hand, considering how many scholars misunderstand or have difficulty explaining what a p-value is (Aschwanden, 2015) or fail to grasp the differences between fixed- and random-effects models (Certo et al., 2017), among many other seemingly innocuous and ostensibly well-grasped empirical procedures, I suspect there is a considerable gap between what should be commonly understood and what actually is. In my experience, I find many scholars, both new and seasoned, fail to take advantage of many of the ideas outlined here when submitting their work. Too many accept statistical significance as "proof" of support for their ideas and hastily push toward submission never considering if that result was luck or the work of statistical anomalies traced to outliers or coding errors. Thus, while the primary audience of this chapter is likely to be those who are relatively new to the field of strategic management (doctoral students and newer faculty), it is my hope that many of the ideas will resonate with and be useful to more seasoned scholars as well.

Moreover, and perhaps even more crucially for our field, I hope these ideas can inform all of us as reviewers. No study is perfect. Rather, every study has lingering weaknesses or slight inconsistencies. Most papers conflict, to some degree, with prior theory or empirical findings. Often there's a result that doesn't quite line up with the rest of the empirical evidence. Research should be judged on the collective merit of the arguments and evidence offered, with some level of acceptance that flaws and inconsistencies will always exist. A body of evidence can paint a broad picture about what might be. Within that body of evidence, inconsistencies or weaknesses create avenues for continued dialogue (Huff, 1999), new research, and eventual breakthroughs (Hollenbeck & Wright, 2017). From this perspective, then, a secondary audience of this chapter might be the more seasoned scholars serving as reviewers or editors and in the privileged position of determining what gets published. Here my hope is that these ideas serve as a counterbalance against our natural tendency to nitpick every small flaw while failing to see how a given study builds on past conversations while opening the door to new ones yet to come.

A BODY OF EVIDENCE

What is a "body of evidence"? Borrowing from criminal justice, when pursuing a criminal case, a prosecutor must present evidence that proves, beyond a reasonable doubt, that a defendant is guilty of a crime. In pursuing this work, the astute prosecutor must identify and lay to rest any alternative and reasonably plausible theory about the events that occurred. This can be accomplished by presenting substantial physical evidence establishing critical facts of the case, the use of witness testimony, and the opinions of experts that might speak to the plausibility of alternative explanations or the chances for error when using scientific techniques to analyze evidence.

As an example, imagine a case of theft where a suspect's fingerprints were found at the scene of a crime where valuables were stolen. Simply demonstrating the existence of the defendant's fingerprints is probably not sufficient to convict. One must show that items were actually stolen and not lost, that it was likely the defendant who stole them, and that it is unlikely the crime was committed by someone else. An astute defense attorney, knowing many other fingerprints were present at the scene, will raise this issue to cast doubt. To counteract this, a skilled prosecutor might anticipate the defense will raise this issue. Rather than wait, the prosecutor might proactively demonstrate they belong to individuals known to be routinely at the scene while also documenting that each has an alibi that reasonably eliminates them from consideration. In doing so, the prosecutor is showing that they questioned their own case.

The parallels aren't perfect. In court, testimony happens in real time and witnesses from each side can be immediately cross examined. In attempting to publish a manuscript, the process is asynchronous, and authors get to respond formally only if a revise and resubmit is offered. Still, an author is akin to the prosecutor presenting a case to the jury (action editor) while a reviewer is the defense attorney for science – a guardian for truth aiming to keep bad science from entering the hallowed pages of our respected journals. A reviewer's job, then, is to identify pockets of reasonable doubt in a manuscript. An author, in turn, must present a body of compelling logical arguments and empirical evidence that provides ample support for the claims made. If an author can effectively foresee the lines of inquiry that are likely to come from reviewers (like the astute prosecutor above), authors can also participate in the cross examination by proactively answering reviewer questions as they turn the pages of a manuscript.

It is not entirely clear to me what the standard of evidence should be. Depending on the maturity of the research topic under consideration and how the findings might affect the health, welfare, or safety of the people, businesses, society, or other relevant entity that is the focus of the study, one could easily argue for a standard of "more likely than not" a hypothesis is true, "beyond a reasonable doubt," or some other standard. Of course, setting that standard is under the purview of reviewers and editors. But, what seems clear to me is that one cannot simply offer a hypothesis, report the result of a single regression model with stars in the appropriate place documenting a p-value of less than 0.05, and then declare victory. More is needed, and this can be accomplished by building a body of evidence.

Below I will discuss some of the elements that can encompass a body of evidence. As summarized in Table 1, these include descriptions of the sample and measures, descriptive statistics, formal hypothesis tests, alternative specifications, supplemental analyses, and examples. Notably, papers do not need to include all of these nor is this an exhaustive list of possible forms of evidence. A body of evidence should

Table 1. Components of a Body of Evidence.

Category	Examples	Purpose
Sample and measures	• Complete description of sample including accounting for lost observations • Clear description of measures • Support for construct validity even for existing measures	• Transparency, future replication, clear understanding that sample reflects population of interest • Ensuring measures meaningfully capture constructs
Descriptive statistics	• Correlations of key relationships • Means with group comparisons • Distributions	• Generate a sense that the data are behaving as expected without fancy, multivariate analyses
Formal tests and effect sizes	• Traditional regression results • Related beta coefficients • Confidence intervals • Marginal effects • Practical or economic impact	• Provide formal statistical support for claimed relationships and demonstration of magnitude
Alternative specifications	• Alternative measures • Varied sampling techniques • Alternative estimators	• Provide robustness to demonstrate relationships were not found due to luck or that the relationship is only found in a very particular sample with certain measures that was picked "because it worked"
Alternative explanations and supplemental tests	• Alternative logical tests that must be true (or not) if your results are true • Tests of the limits of your theoretical arguments	• Test boundary conditions and attempt to rule out alternative arguments and causal mechanisms • Explore novel findings that might generate new conversations
Examples	• Anecdotes • Case studies • Quotes	• Capture the phenomenon of study in the real world • Demonstrate relationship exists and is recognizable
Other creative approaches	• Limited only by creativity of author(s)	• Further tell the story of the paper

be assembled to tell a story, build from existing research conversations (Huff, 1999), flow logically from the theoretical arguments and formal results, and can include an array of creative approaches not covered here. Before getting into the various forms of evidence, I address why formal tests, alone, are often insufficient evidence to fully support theoretical arguments. I then discuss the various forms of evidence. To conclude, I discuss the value of having this dialogue with reviewers and offer suggestions for how an author might gain the foresight needed to anticipate review questions before submitting a paper for review. I also briefly address how reviewers might think about this process as well.

INSUFFICIENCY OF FORMAL TESTS AND THE FOLLY OF OVERINTERPRETING *P*-VALUES

Recall that, for a null-hypothesis test, a *p*-value is simply the odds of finding a relationship as large as was found (or larger) in a given sample when there is no corresponding relationship in the underlying population (Bettis et al., 2016; Kennedy, 2008). Many misinterpret p-values as one or all of the following: the odds a finding is wrong; or one minus the p-value as the odds the finding is true; or an indication of the relative strength of a finding ($p = 0.01$ is "stronger" than $p = 0.05$). These are all commonly applied and wildly incorrect. To further emphasize this, run the Stata code available in Appendix 1. The code generates 100 random "y" variables and 100 random "x" variables and then generates 100 regressions where a single x ($x1, x2, x3...x100$) is used to predict the corresponding y ($y1, y2, y3...y100$). Imagine each x–y pair is a random draw from some large population of interest. Each randomly drawn sample includes 100 observations. In the final step of the Stata code, the betas and p-values for x-variable in the 100 regressions are captured and tallied. The final line outputs a value tabulating the number of times out of the 100 models when the p-value for the x beta was less than or equal to 0.05.

Given the data are randomly generated, the "true" relationship in the underlying population is zero. Yet, by definition, the expected outcome here is five. That is, we'd expect five cases out of 100 where the p-value is less than or equal to 0.05 even if our data were purely random. If you run this code repeatedly (say 100 times), the average number of cases with p-value less than or equal to five will be approximately 5 but individual runs will return values that range well above and below 5. Why does this happen? When randomly generating a sample from the population, sometimes through dumb luck we get a sample that shows a relationship that doesn't exist in the population – a Type 1 error. If our standard is a p-value that is less than or equal to 0.05, then, even with completely random data, we will see statistically significant coefficients approximately five percent of the time. With a critical value of 0.10, the expectation would be 10. In the version I ran as I am typing this, there were 8 with p less than or equal to 0.05 and 12 less than or equal to 0.10 (see Table 2 for a list of these cases). The two lowest p-values were 0.000 and 0.005 corresponding to betas of -0.389 and $+0.297$, respectively. If the two lowest p-values provide "significant"

Table 2. "Significant" ($p \leq 0.10$) Betas and p-Values in 100 Regressions With Random Data.

Case	p-Value	Beta	Confidence Interval	
1.	0.000	−0.389	−0.583	−0.195
2.	0.005	0.297	0.090	0.504
3.	0.014	−0.238	−0.426	−0.050
4.	0.020	−0.237	−0.436	−0.039
5.	0.028	0.205	0.023	0.386
6.	0.031	0.218	0.020	0.416
7.	0.032	−0.193	−0.368	−0.017
8.	0.040	0.184	0.008	0.360
9.	0.068	0.173	−0.013	0.359
10.	0.072	0.162	−0.015	0.340
11.	0.073	0.196	−0.019	0.412
12.	0.078	−0.192	−0.406	0.022

estimates for the population that are similarly sized in magnitude but in the opposite direction, it should be clear why the *p*-value cannot speak to the "strength" of a result.

Understanding how this simple example applies to research highlights a critical reason why we need to build a body of evidence in our papers. With each study we complete, we take a scoop of randomly selected data (we hope it is randomly selected, and for sake of argument here, let's assume it is) from an underlying population and compute statistical tests from that sample. Using the results of these tests on the sample, we estimate or infer – why it's called inferential statistics – what the value of that parameter is in the population. No empirical estimator is perfect. Each has numerous assumptions, and we almost always violate at least some of them. Even if we didn't, it's important to acknowledge that our fancy statistical tools only provide estimates of what is occurring in the population along with a confidence interval of that estimate. But this is not 100% certainty. That is, there's no guarantee the real value lies within the specified range because estimates will offer false positives a nontrivial portion of the time.

As illustrated with my sampling distribution example via the code in Appendix 1, if the 100 pairs of *x* and *y* represented 100 scholars simultaneously but independently pursuing similar research questions with a randomly chosen sample from the same underlying population, we would expect about 5 of them to have supported results with a *p*-value less than or equal to 0.05 even if the relationship didn't exist. If one "significant" test was enough, we would have to concede that our journals are disproportionately filled with the lucky few who found the spurious or random results supportive of hypothesized relationships that do not exist in the population (Goldfarb & King, 2016). We can begin to overcome this problem by building a body of evidence. Authors must accept that reviewers are rightly asking, at least in part, "was this paper one of the 5-in-100 that found a result from luck or is this result real?" Of course, in a cruel bit of irony regarding what it takes to be interesting, with increasingly counterintuitive or novel hypotheses (Davis, 1971), we would expect a reviewer to be increasingly skeptical.

Sadly, *p*-values have been given "almost mythical properties far removed from the mundane probabilistic definition" (Bettis et al., 2016, p. 259) that underlies their correct meaning. A *p*-value of 0.049 is taken to mean that a corresponding hypothesis is "true" yet one that is 0.051 means it is most certainly "false." Of course, in most studies of modest sample sizes, these two *p*-values are certainly not practically or even statistically different from each other. Yet, in many cases, one gains the scientist a publication while the other goes into the file drawer. While beyond the scope of this chapter, alternative approaches do exist. Replications allow us to assess the validity and boundary conditions of prior work, and Bayesian analyses allow us to calculate the degree of belief in an outcome based on our prior knowledge of the topic. Further, the random paper that gets published when the results were spurious should not doom science to the fate desired by skeptics. As Bettis et al. (2016) note, "one study proves little or nothing-...Instead, it establishes initial confirming evidence" (p. 260). In assessing the true nature of the world, we should assess the collective body of scientific evidence.

For this, meta-analytical approaches allow scientists to combine multiple studies which then provide estimates of relationships that have narrower confidence intervals.

One final point on p-values. The role of theory here is critical. Absent theory, a finding with a p-value of 0.05 should be interpreted as I have described above. However, given plausible theory and a p-value of 0.05, we now have a conditional probability, an idea on which Bayesian analyses are fundamentally built. That is, given a theory is plausible and a low p-value (e.g., less than or equal to 0.05), one can place more confidence on the research finding than would be the case without the theory. Thus, offering compelling theory, though not addressed below, can be considered a part of the body of evidence, and should spur greater confidence in our results.

FORMS OF EVIDENCE

In the research context, we build a body of evidence by presenting a compelling case that demonstrates a robust link between our conceptual arguments or hypotheses and the corresponding empirical tests. As discussed above, this evidence should tell a story and flow logically from the arguments of the manuscript. Below I discuss several possible forms of evidence and how they might be used. I start with the sampling process, measures, and descriptive statistics. These are critical as they form the foundation of a study and provide an initial lens into the reliability and transparency of a researcher's efforts. From there, I expand to various empirical approaches that can be included in a body of evidence. This should not be seen as an exhaustive approach, as scholars can and should find creative ways to showcase their ideas and support their work.

Sample and Measures

Most "Empirical Methodology" sections begin with a description of the sample used in the study followed by variable descriptions. Given that the inferences for a population are based on the sample, it is critical that researchers clearly document how the sample was formed, what data sources were used, inclusion or exclusion criteria to make an initial sample, and why any data were removed from an initial sample on the way to a final sample (e.g., random selection, missing data, or exclusion based on theoretical grounds). For example, studies in strategic management focus on specific years and include some industries and not others. Financial services firms report financials in fundamentally different ways and are often excluded from studies as a result. Some studies exclude new firms or firms smaller than a certain size. Still others only focus on firms in a particular stock index (e.g., S&P 500 or 1500). It's critical that scholars clearly articulate the relevant population of interest. Then, they must document the sampling criteria that generated the final sample for a given study. This should include specific counts of cases at the start, how many are dropped in each step, and the final count. Counts should also be provided for any relevant groupings within data. If the study is on CEOs, then counts of unique CEOs, unique firms, and total rows of data should be included. Adding additional sample descriptions such as number of industries, firms by industry, and similar items can be useful as well. All of this allows a reader to understand the nature of the sample relative to a broader population.

In accounting for the sample, it is especially important to address missing data. If your sample is the S&P 500 for a 10-year period, it would be expected that you would have roughly 500 × 10 or 5,000 firm-years. If your final sample includes only 4,000 firm-years and no explanation is offered for the "missing" 1,000 records, it shouldn't be surprising when reviewers react with skepticism. If the base of your sample is Compustat or other commonly available dataset, it is reasonable that a reviewer might even download the dataset and see for themselves what sort of sample they can generate following your description. Any unexplained large discrepancies in sample size will make reviewers increasingly skeptical of everything else.

Related to this, each measure used in a study should be clearly described. If using existing measures, share enough to demonstrate it was done the same way as the original. If there are deviations from prior work, this and the rationale for deviating must be clearly documented. Finally, it is critical that measures convincingly capture the underlying construct they claim to represent. Notably, if a measure is relatively new, and sometimes even if it isn't, construct validity can still be called into question (Boyd et al., 2013; Gove & Junkunc, 2013), so the most prudent authors should offer their own arguments or evidence demonstrating validity.

Descriptive Statistics

In a typical manuscript of 40-pages, the correlation table might take up a full page or roughly 2% of the overall length, yet it is often almost entirely ignored in the text of a paper. That is, the typical "Table 1" of a study is generally mentioned just once at the start of the results section with a sentence such as: "Table 1 displays correlations and descriptive statistics of our sample." But, with this table, authors have a chance to demonstrate the reliability of their data and offer the first bit of evidence in support of their work (or address the first line of potential criticism). First, to generate confidence, researchers can demonstrate that certain values are consistent with prior work. For example, if there is a firm performance measure, its mean and standard deviation (as well as minimum and maximum if reported) should be consistent with prior work with comparable samples.

A similar approach can be taken with correlations. If a study including measures of firm performance and an indicator for CEO termination provides a correlation that is positive (e.g., suggesting good performance leads to termination), reviewers can and should be skeptical. Moving to the hypothesized relationships, if there is a proposed negative link between x and y, one would generally expect there to be at least a modest negative bivariate correlation between these variables as well, assuming unexplained heterogeneity wasn't so pernicious as to invert the direction of the estimated association. As such, one might start the results section of a paper by highlighting such a correlation. If it doesn't exist (or if the relationship is inverted), the author is well-advised to begin addressing the complex relations that create a scenario where the general relationship is positive, but the relationship of interest is still negative. For example, Simpson's paradox (Simpson, 1951) highlights how it is possible for a relationship to exist within subgroup but not exist (or exist in the opposite direction) across groups. Not directly discussing this might doom your paper immediately in the eyes of an observant and skeptical reviewer. Of course, this creates a link to the formal test where, if this paradox existed, one would also have to account for grouping or nesting of data through, for example, multilevel modeling.

Next, one might present additional descriptive statistics relevant to the relationship at hand. Perhaps the hypothesis entails a binary x-variable predicting a continuous outcome such that the $x = 1$ group is expected to have higher values of y than the $x = 0$ group. One can demonstrate this by reporting simple group means for y under the two conditions of x, a common practice in many other disciplines. Alternatively, one could graph the values of y to visually show how one group has consistently higher values than the other.

As an anecdote from my own work, my coauthors and I hypothesized that CEOs hired from outside the firm would deliver more extreme performance than insiders (Quigley et al., 2019). Our first bit of "evidence" demonstrating this was a pair of histograms showing a wider and flatter distribution of outcomes for outsider CEOs and a narrower and taller distribution of outcomes for insiders. If the hypothesized x-variable is continuous, this same sort of descriptive statistics or visual depiction can be created by dividing the x-values into low, medium, and high groups and reporting means or displaying graphical distributions for these groups, or even by producing binned scatterplots (Starr & Goldfarb, 2020). This approach allows a reader to visibly see the claimed relationships in the underlying data before going into more complex analyses. Notably, one could also use this approach to address the issue of Simpson's Paradox. If the relationship is believed to be negative within group but the bivariate correlation in the sample is positive, then graphing by group or reporting the proportion of times the within-group correlation was negative could begin to address the issue.

Formal Tests and Effect Sizes

After these initial descriptive results, one might move to reporting results of formal hypothesis testing using the analytical techniques described in the methods section of a manuscript. While substantial effort might be needed to demonstrate that the model assumptions hold (e.g., reporting instrument validity tests for two-stage modeling or demonstrating reasonable evidence of parallel trends for difference-in-difference modeling, among others), the actual process of reporting results is straightforward. If your hypothesis claimed a negative relationship between x and y, this is demonstrated with a negative coefficient and some level of statistical significance. However, authors can build additional evidence by reporting confidence intervals and, as is now required in *Strategic Management Journal*, by demonstrating the practical and/or economic impact of the reported relationship. If the claim is that increases in your *x*-variable results in a reduction in market valuation in firms, for instance, you can build your body of evidence within the formal econometric test by documenting the average amount of decline that is associated with a one standard deviation change in your independent variable.

You should also consider reporting marginal effects – which represent the differential relationships between the independent and dependent variables over different values of relevant variables – numerically and via graphs, especially when hypothesizing interactions (Busenbark, Graffin, et al., 2022). Simply noting that an interaction was "significant" does not provide a clear picture of the actual relationship, but a graph can. Further, calculating and reporting marginal effects allows an author to describe the size of impact at various levels of the *x*-variable and moderator while noting if the differences are statistically significant and/or practically meaningful. One pitfall that can be easily avoided with this approach is an interaction that is significant but not meaningfully impactful in a reasonable range of the data. For example, perhaps CEO tenure moderates the link between some CEO trait and firm performance. But if the difference only becomes significant or economically important in year 37 of a CEO's tenure, it becomes hard to claim any sort of practical impact given how few CEOs serve that long.

Alternative Specifications

Next, you can consider alternative specifications. That is, in justifying the use of a particular estimator, it is likely that a reasonable case could be made for one or more alternative analytic procedures. For example, while it is common to use random-effects estimators when there is no within-group variance on a key independent variable (for example, when CEO's prior experience, education, or gender is a variable of interest), some reviewers might prefer generalized estimating equations (GEE) or multilevel modeling (MLM). Executing these tests and stating, "Our results were robust to the use of GEE and MLM as well (results available upon request)" generates considerable confidence, especially for a reviewer who might prefer those approaches. Just be sure to properly save those alternative models in the case someone asks for them (and in the review process, you might include them in a response letter or as an appendix).

In some cases, however, you might choose a particular estimator over another commonly used approach because the assumptions of the first are more completely satisfied while there are compelling violations with the other. In these cases, you should rightfully reject the less appropriate tool and explain the choice. But it might also be useful to consider its use to study boundary conditions where changes in the underlying assumptions might yield nuanced findings that prove useful to the field.

Authors can also consider different measures, changes to the sampling approach (including smaller firms, different industries, or additional time periods), shifts in lags for calculating variables across time, or other alternatives. Each of these can demonstrate the robustness and external validity of your results, showing the skeptic that you are questioning your own choices and thus providing some assurances that you didn't just pick the one model that supported your hypotheses out of a myriad that didn't. For example, if the initial sampling frame included removing firms with less than $100 million in revenues, then an alternative model might probe if the results are robust to a cutoff of $500 million or $50 million. Or, if a primary variable is measured as the number of acquisitions in a two-year period, one might test if the results are robust to measurement across one-year or three-years. So long as these more exploratory analyses are conducted openly (rather than repackaged as a priori hypotheses after finding the result), they should be encouraged in the spirit of "THARKING" (transparently hypothesizing after the results are known) rather than SHARKING (secretly hypothesizing after the results are known), as discussed by Hollenbeck and Wright (2017).

Alternative Explanations and Supplemental Tests

You should also step back to consider alternative explanations for your findings and offer empirical tests that attempt to rule these out. Imagine a study linking the personality trait of extroversion in CEOs with a particular firm outcome. Rather than being randomly assigned, it is conceivable that these results were driven by CEOs attracted to a certain opportunity or that they were recruited by the board because their personality was believed to be ideal for navigating the firm a specific way in the current task environment. Or, as research has shown, a prior CEO might be inclined to advocate for the hiring of a new CEO that is similar to themselves (Zajac & Westphal, 1996). The primary test of this relationship will likely include some sort of model to deal with this possible endogeneity. But reviewers may remain skeptical even in the presence of compelling findings from this primary model. Here, creative thinking might allow you to test alterative explanations in hopes of assuaging these reviewer concerns. For example, you might be able to demonstrate variance in the personality of CEOs within a firm (specifically showing that the personality of the outgoing CEOs is different than incoming CEOs), that CEOs coming to firms facing similar internal and external environments exhibit different personality traits and diverging paths once in office, and that the personality traits of CEOs, as measured through archival sources, remain consistent to repeated measurement over time.

None of these tests can "prove" that reviewer concerns are invalid. Still, offering robustness tests, supplemental analysis, and tests of boundary conditions builds the body of evidence and can go a long way toward assuaging reviewer concerns. In some cases, these efforts might yield novel findings that spur further conversations and research. The key here is to step back and consider what a reasonable reviewer might be asking, rhetorically, as they read your work. And rather than let the question go unanswered, you offer an answer to them as they turn the pages of your manuscript.

Examples and Anecdotes

Some scholars take the approach of using mixed-methods to study a phenomenon (e.g., Eisenhardt, 1989). This entails linking two formal studies in a single paper – often one qualitative and the other quantitative. While laudable, doing so is a challenge for some topics and the associated complexity can be limiting for some scholars. At the same time, one can borrow from this approach as a means to generate some realism and support for empirical claims. As a reviewer and associate editor, I have often asked authors to "show me how this looks in the data with a real-world example." What I am requesting is a case where a firm experienced the relationship proposed in the study. Imagine a scenario where one is hypothesizing a within-firm negative relationship between a form of strategic action and future performance. You might document this in a few firms by showing actual data highlighting the expected pattern of strategic choices and then showing the measures for the outcome. If this can be done with anecdotal accounts from news coverage, that would be even more compelling.

Similarly, you might consider using quotes to show plausibility. That is, imagine a study that argues for a particular CEO mindset leading to a certain type of strategic decision. The study might use content analysis of earnings calls to assess CEO mindset and archival accounting performance data for the outcome. To add further evidence, you might find quotes from an interview of a CEO clearly demonstrating the mindset prior to a decision you expect is associated with that mindset. Done well, a researcher can demonstrate the existence and plausibility of a phenomenon using concrete examples. Though I mention this item last, I believe this approach can be used throughout a paper to demonstrate theory in action which can help readers more fully and clearly understand conceptual arguments.

Other Issues and Creative Approaches

Endogeneity is among the most common concerns for strategic management studies (Hamilton & Nickerson, 2003). While instrumental variables and various forms of two-stage models allow authors to deflect some of this criticism, authors can further address this through one or more techniques recently introduced to the management literature. One approach is the impact threshold of a confounding variable test (ITCV) (Busenbark, Yoon, et al., 2022; Frank, 2000). With endogeneity, there is unmeasurable confounding variance related to both the independent and dependent variables which, if included in a model, might negate a result. The ITCV allows one to quantify the size of the correlations needed between potentially missing (and unmeasurable) variables and both the key variables to invalidate the results. By comparing the size of this correlation with the size of known correlations between variables that are in the model, it is often possible to make the case that an omitted variable with the needed correlations is quite unlikely (Busenbark, Yoon, et al., 2022).

There are other approaches that offer sensitivity analyses that are similar to the ITCV. Oster (2019), for example, offers a test that calculates a bias-adjusted estimate given the impact of control variables and level of unexplained variance. Similarly, Cinelli and Hazlett (2020) offer a tool that "shows how strongly confounders explaining all the residual outcome variation would have to be associated with the treatment to eliminate the estimated effect" (p. 39). The point is, even after addressing endogeneity (or perhaps in cases where instruments for addressing endogeneity simply aren't available), these tools allow you to go a step further and quantify how large the problem would have to be to invalidate results. While you can never eliminate the possibility that confounding variance would invalidate an inference, these tests can at least help quantify the hazard.

Outliers are also problematic for strategic management research, especially in studies using archival financial data. Specifically, reviewers often wonder if a small number of influential observations might be driving results. To demonstrate this, consider the code in Appendix 2. It generates 1,000 random values of x and y and then regresses y on x. Like the earlier example, since this is purely random data, we would not expect a significant coefficient. But, due to chance in the sampling process, roughly 1 in 20 attempts will generate a p-value for x that is less than or equal to 0.05. But, if just a few outliers exist in this otherwise random data (in this case I define just four additional cases), the coefficients for x have p-values less than or equal to 0.05 almost every time. While Winsorizing and other transformations remain common but fallible remedies, authors might consider building on their body of evidence through others means. If a relationship is expected across the range of x and y values, consider dropping a small number of cases at the extremes of key variables to see if reported results remain robust. If a relationship only exists when the four most extreme cases are included, it is probably warranted to reconsider the strength of the empirical evidence.

ANTICIPATING QUESTIONS AND OVERCOMING SKEPTICISM
The Benefits of Building a Body of Evidence

If you successfully anticipate questions asked by reviewers, it is useful to then consider what this achieves. You, as an author, have spent months or years painstakingly developing theory, crafting hypotheses, building your dataset, and completing statistical analyses. If this research project is truly a new contribution to the literature, it is likely no one else in the world knows as much about the nuances of the topic and the underlying data as you (this should especially be the case if this effort is a product of your dissertation). While reviewers might be experts in the general domain, it's unlikely they have the same knowledge as you, the author, about this particular topic, setting, or the key concepts at the center of your work.

Imagine a reviewer gets deep into your manuscript and asks the question "but did you consider <fill in the topic>?" The reviewer then flips the page only to find a passage that says, "...of course a reasonable criticism of our work is that <fill in the topic> might be affecting our results. To address this concern, we..." As the author, you might go on to say, "Building on this issue, it's also important to consider these three related issues, A, B, and C which we also addressed as follows..." Imagine the response of a reviewer at that point. They probably smile and even relax a little bit. They feel some pride in catching an issue that you quickly address and nod in agreement when you note the three additional issues related to the first. Why? While you, the author, have spent months or years on this project, the reviewer is maybe 30 minutes or an hour into it. Yet, by anticipating and answering the reviewer's question, you are engaging them in a powerful way even though the communication is asynchronous. In answering the reviewer question as it was asked, you are tacitly acknowledging the reviewer's intellect. You are also assuring them that they understand where you are going, thus leveraging the reviewer's confirmation bias to your benefit. This engagement creates positive rapport between you and the reviewer at a critical moment of the review process. In the moment skepticism was going to creep in, you stunted it by effectively anticipating and then answering the questions. The affective, explicit, and subconscious benefits of this asynchronous conversation cannot be overstated.

Anticipating Reviewer Questions

But how do you anticipate the multitude of possible questions reviewers might ask so you can address them proactively? You might even think, "sure, I can think of 3 or 4 things, but reviewers seemingly invent a thousand reasons to hate my work." As an author, I can assure you I've felt that exact emotion before. But, as an associate editor, one of the more compelling realizations I've had is how often reviewers have considerable overlap on the major concerns that result in a paper getting rejected. My argument is that you can anticipate these, perhaps with some help, before submitting your paper.

The first step here is to critically evaluate your own work to identify potential weaknesses or alternative explanations and then addressing them as best you can. To aid in this process, scholars should marshal assistance from a variety of sources. For example, simply talking with colleagues about your work over coffee or lunch can often generate multiple lines of potential inquiry. Doing this while you are developing your research plan allows you to incorporate the feedback into the study design. Data needed for this can then be gathered up front rather than afterwards when it is more costly to do so.

As you develop the manuscript, you can gain insights from peers through presentations in seminars or informal "brown bag" sessions in your own department or during visits to other universities. The value here can be multifaceted. First, committing your project to a presentation forces you to fully explain your ideas in ways you have yet to do, and this might allow you to uncover previously unseen weaknesses or omissions in your conceptual arguments or empirics. Second, sharing these ideas to a new group might uncover novel ideas to enhance your study, such as additional moderators, novel measures, or important controls. These audiences might also raise important questions that can be addressed using some of the types of evidence discussed above (particularly alternative specifications and supplemental analyses). Addressing these now adds to the likelihood that you might answer one of the eventual reviewers' questions thereby eliminating a potential line of criticism.

Perhaps you are at a point in your career where it is unlikely you will receive an invitation to present or in a department where internal presentations aren't common. If so, propose to create such a forum and offer to be the first presenter. If you are still a student, work within your cohort at your university and present informally to one and other. You might even seek out those in adjoining fields to join you. Students and junior faculty can also create informal groups of colleagues from other universities and meet virtually a few times a year via Zoom. I have personally benefitted from arrangements such as these long before I was ever invited to present at another university.

Once a manuscript is fully developed, submission to conferences creates an opportunity for even more feedback. Moreover, in this setting it is likely that one or more future reviewers of your work might be in attendance when you present. Imagine getting specific feedback at a conference, addressing it in your manuscript, and then that person becomes Reviewer 2 on your submitted paper. Imagine this reviewer recalls the paper, remembers giving the comment, and then seeing this issue addressed based on their ideas. It seems this could only help the odds of getting a revision opportunity. Even the prototypically menacing "Reviewer 2" is likely to be gratified by seeing their own idea in place. It could also be the case that this reviewer doesn't remember the presentation or giving the comment but, given how our brains work, that reviewer is likely to have the same criticism reading your work as they did in your presentation. Addressing their comment will still have a compelling positive effect. Of course, this does not mean you should implement every idea you are given. The discerning scholar needs to be the expert within their domain and pick and choose which feedback to address accordingly.

Another step of gaining insights to lingering weaknesses in your manuscript is the friendly review. Once a paper is, in your mind, ready for submission to a journal, you then send it out to peers for friendly evaluation. This would preferably be scholars familiar with the broad theories you employ, but not familiar with your specific study. At this point you might think "I've spent 500 hours on this project, shared it with peers at brown bags, presented it at conferences, and poured over the results and writing for dozens of revisions. . .I need to get it under review, and can't afford another month of delay." Yet, the value of gaining feedback from respected scholars is tremendous. Imagine if you could send your paper to a journal once, get feedback, address those issues, and then send it back to that journal again with a fresh start. How much might this improve your prospects? This is essentially a friendly review, especially if you can lean on friends who routinely review for the journal you are targeting.

Let's say a friendly review spots a few issues you can address with some additional empirical tests and by simply clarifying your writing in a few places. Imagine this adds a month to the process but makes the difference between a reject and an R&R. Is it worth it? Of course, and this is why all the most successful senior scholars I know, including those with dozens of A-level publications, always share papers with friends before sending out to a journal. Just make sure you pick friends who agree to give you quick feedback and who aren't afraid of telling you the truth. The more effective you can be at anticipating questions from reviewers and providing answers to those questions in the manuscript as part of your body of evidence, the better your chances are with the review team.

One final thought that can really enhance your body of evidence. Consider sharing some or all your data and/or code. In the coming years, some form of this will probably become the norm in many of our journals. Scholars who get into the habit of conducting their research such that their code and data are properly organized and ready to be shared will have an advantage. Until then, those who willingly share even portions of code or data demonstrate a commitment to open science and transparency that generates more confidence in the body of evidence than any other example offered here.

JOURNAL AND REVIEWER CONSIDERATIONS

Online Appendices

While incorporating any one of these suggestions will add negligible length to a manuscript, adding several to create a substantial body of evidence is likely to create challenges adhering the page length limits at most journals. Traditionally, authors were simply forced to cut content to maintain page lengths at something that could be published. Today, however, journals, editors, and reviewers are more welcoming of appendices, intended to be published online, that provide supplemental materials. Such appendices can contain additional descriptions of a complex aspect of your methods, sample details, robustness tests, or other materials. While it would be inaccurate to say that space is now unlimited (for example, reviewers still need to assess the veracity of supplemental materials), it is possible to briefly note something in a manuscript while providing more complete details shifted to an online appendix.

Thoughts for the Reviewer

It is also useful to consider how this plays out from the perspective of reviewers and editors. I started out this chapter by arguing that authors should create a body of evidence while also noting that not every test works out perfectly. Some supplemental tests might return p-values that are above common thresholds of statistical significance. Imagine an author reporting a significant correlation, a primary test with a p-value less than or equal to 0.05, meaningful effect sizes, and a few supplemental tests that are significant at common levels, but also one alternative test of the primary model where the coefficient p-value is 0.08. Authors should not shy away from reporting these results and, if the estimates remain reasonable, reviewers should take them for what they are: additional support offered as part of a body of evidence. Rather than recommending a rejection based on one test above the commonly used, but arbitrary, threshold of 0.05, reviewers and editors should consider the full body of evidence. After all, as noted above, it is most likely the case that a pair of p-values, one slightly above and another slightly below common levels of statistical significance, are not meaningfully different from each other.

More broadly, reviewers and action editors should be open to the inconsistencies and messiness of research as a means to extend conversations (and the related research) into areas that help us further understand the phenomenon of interest. If a paper presents results that are otherwise trustworthy and interesting but, in some way, at odds with existing work – or if a paper has strong findings but some unanswered questions that can be addressed by future work – it seems reasonable to support publication so the discussion can continue, rather than reject because of an inconsistency or unanswered question. Reviewers should frequently ask themselves "is it reasonable for a single paper to do yet one more thing" or is it better to allow the conversation to continue by publishing a study knowing that a community of scholars can then wrestle with an inconsistency, conduct additional studies, and, over time, address concerns or open questions that remain. It's a balancing act but, when reviewing, it is a question we should all ask ourselves as an effective counterbalance against the ever-growing expectation that authors do more and more in a single manuscript. Rather than asking for more or rejecting over small inconsistencies or lingering questions, it may be better to publish which allows conversations to flourish through later studies conducted by a wider array of scholars. In my view, so long as the underlying scholarship is sound and trustworthy, this will ultimately lead to the generation of more knowledge over time. However, if an inconsistency or open question is the result of sloppy scholarship, or if a glaring weakness goes completely unaddressed, it is reasonable to expect criticism and a resulting rejection.

CONCLUSION

In the early days of the field of strategic management, manuscripts were often published that tested hypotheses with a single model that relied heavily on reporting statistical significance via p-values. Effect sizes were often not discussed, and few, if any, supplemental tests or alternative specifications offered. Today, reviewers are demanding greater evidence that a study's empirical findings are robust. In this chapter, I outlined the idea of a "body of evidence" and offered some guidance for how scholars might develop more compelling compendium of results in support of their ideas. The process entails anticipating critical questions from reviewers and answering them as part of the initial submission. In doing so, authors can engage in an asynchronous dialogue that builds rapport with reviewers (and eventual readers) while the resulting transparency generates trust in the research process. Authors can build their body of evidence by focusing a critical lens on their own work and by gaining feedback through discussions with colleagues, presentations, and friendly reviews. It is my belief that pursuing this approach will result in greater chances of paper acceptance for authors, better experiences for reviewers, and stronger science for the field.

REFERENCES

Aschwanden, C. (2015). *Not even scientists can easily explain P-values*. https://fivethirtyeight.com/features/not-even-scientists-can-easily-explain-p-values/. Accessed on February 15, 2023.

Bettis, R. A., Ethiraj, S., Gambardella, A., Helfat, C., & Mitchell, W. (2016). Creating repeatable cumulative knowledge in strategic management: A call for a broad and deep conversation among authors, referees, and editors. *Strategic Management Journal*, 257–261.

Boyd, B. K., Bergh, D. D., Ireland, R. D., & Ketchen, D. J., Jr. (2013). Constructs in strategic management. *Organizational Research Methods*, 16(1), 3–14.

Busenbark, J. R., Graffin, S. D., Campbell, R. J., & Lee, E. Y. (2022). A marginal effects approach to interpreting main effects and moderation. *Organizational Research Methods*, 25(1), 147–169.

Busenbark, J. R., Yoon, H., Gamache, D. L., & Withers, M. C. (2022). Omitted variable bias: Examining management research with the impact threshold of a confounding variable (ITCV). *Journal of Management*, 48(1), 17–48.

Certo, S. T., Busenbark, J. R., Woo, H. S., & Semadeni, M. (2016). Sample selection bias and Heckman models in strategic management research. *Strategic Management Journal*, 37(13), 2639–2657.

Certo, S. T., Withers, M. C., & Semadeni, M. (2017). A tale of two effects: Using longitudinal data to compare within- and between-firm effects. *Strategic Management Journal*, 38(7), 1536–1556.

Cinelli, C., & Hazlett, C. (2020). Making sense of sensitivity: Extending omitted variable bias. *Journal of the Royal Statistical Society: Series B (Statistical Methodology)*, 82(1), 39–67.

Colquitt, J. A., & George, G. (2011). Publishing in AMJ—Part 1: Topic choice. *Academy of Management Journal*, 54(3), 432–435.

Crane, D. (1967). The gatekeepers of science: Some factors affecting the selection of articles for scientific journals. *The American Sociologist*, 195–201.

Davis, M. S. (1971). That's interesting! Towards a phenomenology of sociology and a sociology of phenomenology. *Philosophy of the Social Sciences*, 1(2), 309–344.

Eisenhardt, K. (1989). Making fast strategic decisions in high-velocity environments. *Academy of Management Journal*, 32(3), 543–576.

Frank, K. A. (2000). Impact of a confounding variable on a regression coefficient. *Sociological Methods & Research*, 29(2), 147–194.

Goldfarb, B., & King, A. A. (2016). Scientific apophenia in strategic management research: Significance tests & mistaken inference. *Strategic Management Journal*, 37(1), 167–176.

Gove, S., & Junkunc, M. (2013). Dummy constructs? Binomial categorical variables as representations of constructs: CEO duality through time. *Organizational Research Methods*, 16(1), 100–126.

Hamilton, B. H., & Nickerson, J. A. (2003). Correcting for endogeneity in strategic management research. *Strategic Organization*, 1(1), 51–78.

Hollenbeck, J. R., & Wright, P. M. (2017). Harking, sharking, and tharking: Making the case for post hoc analysis of scientific data. *Journal of Management*, 43(1), 5–18.

Huff, A. S. (1999). *Writing for scholarly publication*. SAGE Publications.

Kennedy, P. (2008). *A guide to econometrics* (6th ed.). Wiley.

Miller, C. C. (2006). Peer review in the organizational and management sciences: Prevalence and effects of reviewer hostility, bias, and dissensus. *Academy of Management Journal*, 49(3), 425–431.

Oster, E. (2019). Unobservable selection and coefficient stability: Theory and evidence. *Journal of Business & Economic Statistics*, 37(2), 187–204.

Quigley, T. J., Hambrick, D. C., Misangyi, V. F., & Rizzi, G. A. (2019). CEO selection as risk-taking: A new vantage on the debate about the consequences of insiders versus outsiders. *Strategic Management Journal*, 40(9), 1453–1470.

Semadeni, M., Withers, M. C., & Trevis Certo, S. (2014). The perils of endogeneity and instrumental variables in strategy research: Understanding through simulations. *Strategic Management Journal*, 35(7), 1070–1079.

Simpson, E. H. (1951). The interpretation of interaction in contingency tables. *Journal of the Royal Statistical Society: Series B*, 13(2), 238–241.

Starbuck, W. H. (2003). Turning lemons into lemonade: Where is the value in peer reviews?. *Journal of Management Inquiry*, 12(4), 344–351.

Starr, E., & Goldfarb, B. (2020). Binned scatterplots: A simple tool to make research easier and better. *Strategic Management Journal*, *41*(12), 2261–2274.

Tihanyi, L. (2020). *From "that's interesting" to "that's important"*. Academy of Management Briarcliff Manor.

Zajac, E. J., & Westphal, J. D. (1996). Who shall succeed? How CEO board preferences and power affect the choice of new CEOs. *Academy of Management Journal*, *39*(1), 64–90.

APPENDIX 1. STATA CODE FOR RANDOM DATA REGRESSIONS

Code downloadable from:
https://timquigley.com/rmsm-code/

```
clear
//set the number of observations
set obs 1000
//create a variable in dataset to capture betas, p-values, and confidence
interval
gen b = .
gen p = .
gen ci_l = .
gen ci_h = .
//loop from 1 to 100
forvalues i = 1/100 {
    gen y`i' = rnormal() //generate y1 through y100
    gen x`i' = rnormal() //generate x1 through x100
    reg y`i' x`i' //run regression predicting y_i with x_i
    mat b=r(table) //save results table
    replace b = b[1,1] if _n==`i' //capture the b-value of the i-th model
    and save to i-th row
    replace p = b[4,1] if _n==`i' // p-value
    replace ci_l = b[5,1] if _n==`i' //low side of confidence interval
    replace ci_h = b[6,1] if _n==`i' // high side of confidence interval
}
//count how many p-values are == 0.05
count if p<=.05
```

APPENDIX 2. STATA CODE FOR OUTLIER EXAMPLE

```
clear
set obs 100
gen y = rnormal()
gen x = rnormal()
reg y x // significant at p<=0.05 ~ 1 in 20
```

```
set obs 104 //add 4 more observations to the data

//Generate the 4 outliers
replace y = 2.5 in 101
replace x = 2.5 in 101
replace y = -3.0 in 102
replace x = -3.5 in 102
replace y = 3.5 in 103
replace x = 3.0 in 103
replace y = -2.5 in 104
replace x = -2.5 in 104

reg y x //significant at p<=0.05 nearly every time
scatter y x
```

PHILOSOPHY AND MANAGEMENT RESEARCH: A CRUCIAL YET NEGLECTED CONNECTION

Eric W. K. Tsang

University of Texas at Dallas, USA

ABSTRACT

Consciously or unconsciously, every management researcher adopts a certain philosophical perspective. In this chapter, I discuss the connection between philosophy and management research and show how philosophical perspectives affect the perception of empirical phenomena, choice of research methods, and interpretation of research results. The discussion indicates that the connection is far more crucial than what many management researchers may have thought. I then share my experience of studying philosophy and provide suggestions to those who are interested in enhancing their knowledge of the subject.

Keywords: Philosophy; research methodology; management research; critical realism; ontology; epistemology

INTRODUCTION

When management researchers hear the term "methodology" or "research methods," they probably think of statistical modeling, sampling, or data collection. Rarely will they associate such terms with philosophy. To management researchers, philosophy is likely to be a recondite subject related only remotely to management research. Yet the simple fact is that consciously or unconsciously, every management researcher adopts a certain philosophical perspective.[1] Philosophy and management research are related in at least two ways – ontological and epistemological. Researchers' beliefs about the fundamental nature of the management phenomena they investigate reflect their ontological commitment. While ontology is concerned with the entities that

Delving Deep
Research Methodology in Strategy and Management, Volume 15, 23–42
Copyright © 2025 Eric W. K. Tsang
Published under exclusive licence by Emerald Publishing Limited
ISSN: 1479-8387/doi:10.1108/S1479-838720240000015002

constitute reality (in which phenomena are observed), including their categori-
zation and relations, epistemology is concerned with how researchers acquire
and process knowledge, as well as how they create and justify their knowledge
claims. Researchers' ontological commitment influences their epistemological
orientation and, together, their ontological and epistemological stances affect
which methods they consider to be legitimate and appropriate when conducting
empirical research (Tsang, 2017).

More than three centuries ago, Locke (1996 [1689], p. 3) maintained that
philosophy could be "employed as the under-laborer in cleaning a little, and
removing some of the rubbish, that lies in the way to knowledge" when he
described the relationship between philosophy and science. In other words,
philosophy assists empirical research by removing whatever obstacles are deemed
to be standing in the way of progress (Bhaskar, 1978). Similar to, but much older
than, Locke's under-laborer analogy is Socrates's midwife analogy. In a long
passage of the *Theaetetus*, Socrates uses the analogy to depict his work as assisting
people to give birth to the wisdom that resides within themselves (Benardete,
2006). Applying these two analogies to the context of management research,
philosophy's function is to help scholars use their wisdom to tackle problems they
encounter in their research process. Stated in more concrete terms, a philosophical perspective is something from which research designs and methods can
be developed and with which they can be aligned (Brown et al., 2021). Philosophy
deals with issues that are more fundamental than, say, the selection of a statistical
modeling method to process a specific dataset for testing a specific hypothesis. So
fundamental are these issues that management researchers sometimes are
unaware of them; their unconsciously adopted philosophical stance has suggested implicitly a way of dealing with the issues.

In this chapter, I discuss the connection between philosophy and management
research and show how philosophical perspectives affect the perception of
empirical phenomena, choice of research methods, and interpretation of research
results. This structure of discussion reflects a typical research process.
Researchers usually start with observing a phenomenon. After deciding that the
phenomenon is worth investigating, the next step is to work out the research
methodology and carry out data collection and analysis procedures. The final
step is to interpret the results. In the following discussion, I show how philosophy
affects these steps.

Owing to space limitations, my discussion covers briefly some of the key
aspects of the philosophy–management research connection for the sake of
showing that the relationship is far more crucial than what many management
researchers may have thought. Needless to say, my discussion is not intended
to provide any methodological guidance. Although I subscribe to realism (or
critical realism to be specific) which sets the tone for this paper, I attempt to
take a more balanced approach, incorporating ideas from different philosophical perspectives. As a backdrop to the discussion, I very briefly compare
between empiricism, positivism, constructivism, and critical realism in the next
section.

A BRIEF COMPARISON OF MAJOR
PHILOSOPHICAL PERSPECTIVES

This section captures the basic points of tension between empiricism, positivism, constructivism, and critical realism along the ontological and epistemological dimensions (Table 1). A caveat is that (1) the boundaries among the four perspectives are far from clear-cut and that (2) no one perspective represents a set of homogenous or even harmoniously coexisting positions. For the first point, there is, for example, a substantial ontological overlap between empiricism and positivism. As to the second, there are often distinct variants within the same perspective. For instance, there are different versions of realism (Harré, 1986), and different schools of thought are clustered under the banner of empiricism (Van Fraassen, 2008). In sum, the discussion here is broad-brush and is not meant to be precise.

To start with, empiricism assumes an objective reality "out there," with the presupposition that "only the actual is possible" (Ayers, 1968, p. 6). There is an emphasis on material existence, and things that are considered existing must be empirically observable. Empiricists adopt the Humean conception of causality which treats the constant conjunction of events as an indicator of a causal relationship. Hume's argument is elaborated in the next section. Empiricism is

Table 1. Comparison of Empiricism, Positivism, Constructivism, and Critical Realism.

	Empiricism	Positivism	Constructivism	Critical Realism
Ontology	Reality is objective with causality conceived as a constant conjunction of events.	Reality is objective with causality conceived as a constant conjunction of events.	Reality is socially constructed through subjective meanings, shared language, and social politics. Agents can willingly create their own realities, and thus, multiple realities are possible.	Reality is objective and stratified, consisting of structures, mechanisms, and events.
Epistemology	The human mind is born with a "blank slate," and knowledge is acquired through sensory experience. Hypotheses and theories must be tested against observations.	Testing and verification of theories is based on a hypothetico-deductive approach, with an aim of discovering law-like relationships that have predictive power.	Knowledge is produced by particular language games. Pluralism and fragmentation are accepted, and contradictory interpretations of the same external reality can be considered equally valid.	Explanations are retroduced from empirical data for describing the structures and mechanisms that generate the observable events. The focus is on explanation rather than prediction.

associated with the "blank slate" conception concerning the origin of knowledge, according to which the human mind is "blank" (i.e., without any innate ideas) at birth and acquires knowledge only through sensory experience (visual, auditory, tactile, gustatory, and olfactory sensation). In other words, all knowledge is *a posteriori*. Scientific knowledge should be derived only or primarily from sensory experience. Hypotheses and theories must be tested against observations.

Similar to empiricism, logical positivism (referred to as positivism throughout this chapter) also assumes the existence of an objective, mind-independent reality and adopts the Humean conception of causality.[2] The main difference lies in epistemology where positivism further develops empiricist principles. Following Hempel's (1965) covering-law model of explanation, positivists adopt a hypothetico-deductive approach and aim at discovering law-like relationships among a set of empirically measurable constructs that have predictive power. The covering-law model upholds a *logic* of scientific explanation; that is, the explanandum (i.e., that which is explained) should be logically deducible from a set of explanans (i.e., that which does the explaining) that include general laws (Douglas, 2009).

In contrast with empiricism and positivism, constructivism views reality as socially constructed via subjective meanings, shared language, and social politics (Berger & Luckmann, 1967). It takes a relativist position in which agents can willingly create their own realities and multiple realities are possible. Drawing on Wittgenstein's (1958) notion of language games, constructivists regard knowledge as produced by agents engaging in particular language games in specific contexts and thus accept pluralism and fragmentation. Constructivists recognize the role played by researchers in shaping and interpreting their findings and may consider contradictory interpretations of the same external reality equally valid.

Similar to empiricism and positivism, critical realism, which is probably the most popular version of realism in management research, assumes an objective reality, but unlike empiricism and positivism, the reality is stratified, consisting of structures and mechanisms that generate events observed in our daily lives (Bhaskar, 1978). Using the method of retroduction, researchers probe into ever-deepening layers of reality and attempt to construct theories that describe the structures and mechanisms responsible for generating the observable events. In contrast with the positivist stress on discovering law-like relationships that have predictive power, realists are content with adequate explanations of past events (Sayer, 1992).

PERCEPTION OF EMPIRICAL PHENOMENA

How one investigates the external world depends on how one perceives that world. This perception in turn depends on one's philosophical perspective. Hume's famous empiricist view of causation is an excellent illustration. Hume's (1999) argument begins with an everyday example − colliding billiard balls − that shows clearly cause and effect. Suppose we observe a blue ball rolling toward a stationary green ball and the blue ball coming into contact with the green ball.

Then, we see the green ball rolling away from the spot where it was struck. At the same time, we also hear a noise when the two balls come into contact. The question is: Do we see a connection between the two events (i.e., the collision of the balls and the ensuing motion of the green ball)? Hume's answer is a resounding "no," with his reasoning summarized in the following passage:

> All events seem entirely loose and separate. One event follows another; but we never can observe any tie between them. They seem *conjoined*, but never *connected*. And as we can have no idea of any thing which never appeared to our outward sense or inward sentiment, the necessary conclusion *seems* to be, that we have no idea of connexion or power at all, and that these words are absolutely without any meaning, when employed either in philosophical reasonings, or common life. (p. 144)

Hume maintains that our idea of necessary connection or power is derived from an internal impression. After we have observed that an event of a certain kind is always followed by an event of another kind, we begin to infer, upon observing an event of the first kind, that an event of the second kind will follow. That is to say, the idea of necessary connection arises from our experience of constant conjunction through observing many similar pairs of events.[3]

It goes without saying that Hume's conception of causation as constant conjunctions of events has important implications for empirical research. Suppose a researcher notices from her longitudinal dataset of restaurants in a big city that whenever a restaurant increases its charitable donation to the local community by at least 10%, its sales revenue will increase by at least 3% in the following year. Adopting an empiricist perspective and thus subscribing to Hume's conception of causation, the researcher would conclude that increasing charitable donations causes the rise in sales revenue.

In contrast, if the researcher is a critical realist and subscribes to a mechanism-based conception of causation, she would not jump to that conclusion. Put simply, "a mechanism is the series of activities of entities that bring about the finish or termination conditions in a regular way" (Machamer et al., 2000, p. 7); for instance, mechanical clocks and electric clocks are based on very different mechanisms to tell time. Returning to our restaurant example, in order to conclude that an increase in donations is a cause of an increase in sales revenue, the researcher must look for a mechanism or mechanisms connecting the two sets of events. One plausible mechanism is that when a restaurant significantly increases its donations to the local community, its public image among residents in the community improves, thus attracting more patronage. To confirm this mechanism, the researcher needs to, say, conduct a survey of the residents or interview them directly. In sum, critical realists attempt to peer into the black box of causality whereas empiricists find no justification for believing that the black box even exists.

Another example – the debate about the ontological nature of entrepreneurial opportunities – illustrates beautifully how philosophy matters in guiding empirical research. Common sense says that things in our world have different modes of existence; the chair I am sitting on exists in a mode that is different from that of the money (as represented by bank notes) in my wallet. The debate was initiated more than two decades ago by Shane and Venkataraman's (2000) seminal article, in which they argue that the defining feature of entrepreneurial phenomena is "the discovery and exploitation of profitable opportunities" (p. 217) and that the objective existence of entrepreneurial opportunities offers a solid foundation for entrepreneurship as a distinctive domain of research. They define entrepreneurial opportunities as "those situations in which new goods, services, raw materials, and organizing methods can be introduced and sold at greater than their cost of production" (p. 220). In other words, entrepreneurial opportunities must be profitable. This feature of profitability is in line with people's usual conception of business opportunities because it makes no sense to say that one has discovered (or created) an opportunity to lose money.[4]

Since its appearance in literature, the *discovery* view of opportunities has been challenged by scholars dissatisfied with the idea that opportunities exist objectively "out there" in ways visible to potential entrepreneurs (McMullen et al., 2007). The challenge developed to such an extreme extent that some scholars denied categorically that opportunities are pre-existing entities in the external world and argued instead that opportunities are created endogenously through entrepreneurial agency (Wood & McKinley, 2010). This camp's core idea is that "opportunities do not exist until entrepreneurs create them through a process of enactment" (Alvarez et al., 2013, p. 307). Such a *creation* approach stresses human agency in entrepreneurial activities.

Stratos Ramoglou and I found that both the empiricist-based discovery view and the constructivist-based creation view have fatal flaws. We therefore adopted a realist perspective and proposed an *actualization* approach that rehabilitates ontologically the objectivity of entrepreneurial opportunities by elucidating their propensity mode of existence. We defined entrepreneurial opportunity as "the propensity of market demand to be actualized into profits through the introduction of novel products or services" (Ramoglou & Tsang, 2016, p. 411). Although both the discovery view and our own view take an objective stance of existence, our actualization view posits that opportunities exist akin to a flower seed's propensity to germinate into a flower versus the flower itself, whereas the discovery view regards opportunities as something like flowers waiting to be discovered. For the actualization view, there are three ways potential entrepreneurs might have cognitive contact with opportunities: (1) *imagining* the state of the world where one makes profits by engaging in an entrepreneurial course of action; (2) *believing* that this state of the world is ontologically possible; (3) after the realization of profits, *knowing* retrospectively that the opportunity in question was truly there. In other words, the only occasion where we can know that an opportunity really exists is at the realization of profits; in the case of failure, we are agnostic.

The debate between the three views is not just an abstract, pedantic matter; it has concrete implications for entrepreneurship research. This can be illustrated by the famous (or perhaps infamous) case of Theranos − the high-flying but ultimately failed biotech start-up that attempted to revolutionize blood testing by inexpensively performing dozens of tests based on a single finger-prick. Theranos is described as "Silicon Valley's greatest startup disaster" (Roy, 2021). The trial of its former CEO and founder, Elizabeth Holmes, that ended in early January 2022, drew a great deal of media attention; Holmes was found guilty by the jury on four charges of defrauding investors. Let's conduct a thought experiment and rewind our clock to around 2013–2014 when Theranos was at its peak and valued at about US$9 billion and Holmes, being the world's youngest billionaire, was not only an entrepreneur but also a celebrity, appearing on the cover of such magazines as *Forbes* and *Fortune*.

Suppose a researcher wants to conduct an intensive case study of Theranos. If he is a follower of the discovery approach, he would deem that Holmes has discovered an opportunity and set up Theranos to exploit it. Note that Shane and Venkataraman (2000) call attention to the puzzling state of affairs that only a handful of entrepreneurs "respond to the situational cues of opportunities" (p. 219). Shane and Venkataraman use the notion of "individual differences" (p. 223) to explain the fact that it is only a few within a larger group who exploit discovered opportunities. Thus, one of the researcher's key research questions would be: Why did Holmes but not others discover and exploit the opportunity? In contrast, if the researcher is a fan of the creation view, he would consider Holmes as the creator of opportunity. One direction of research would be to investigate the stages of opportunity creation, including "conceptualization of an opportunity idea by an entrepreneur, objectification of that idea, and enactment of the opportunity into a new venture" (Wood & McKinley, 2010, p. 66). Finally, if the researcher adopts the actualization approach, he would hold an agnostic stance as to whether Holmes's *imagined* business opportunity exists because Theranos has not been profitable. At that moment, what is confirmed is that Holmes seems to *believe* that the opportunity does exist. Her belief is so strong that she quit Stanford to establish Theranos. Some promising research questions would be: What caused her to come up with that imagined opportunity? What supported her strong belief in the existence of the opportunity? How did she convince investors that the opportunity was real and was not just her imagination? Why did these investors believe her?

With the benefit of hindsight, both the discovery and creation views are seriously flawed in that given the state of blood testing technology at that time (Carreyrou, 2020), it could be concluded safely that the business opportunity that Holmes came up with simply never existed (and in fact, does not exist even now). As such, there was nothing to be discovered, period. As to the creation view, it was simply impossible for Holmes to have created a nonexistent opportunity. Rather, what she had actually created was a company called Theranos, nothing more, nothing less. An entrepreneurial opportunity and a new venture are completely different concepts; creating the latter does not imply creating the former. The actualization view, in contrast, does not commit this error. It suggests the most fruitful agenda to the researcher because it gives the most accurate description of the ontological nature of opportunities among the three views. This thought experiment indicates not only the impact of philosophical perspectives on empirical research but also the importance of adopting a well-reasoned perspective.

CHOICE OF RESEARCH METHODS

The first decision concerning the choice of research method is between the two major categories of research method, namely qualitative and quantitative. Here, qualitative research means "any kind of research that produces findings not arrived at by means of statistical procedures or other means of quantification" (Strauss & Corbin, 1990, p. 17). The emphasis is on the absence of quantitative analysis other than simple statistical tabulation. In contrast, quantitative research refers to studies that focus on quantitative analysis of data, although such studies occasionally contain qualitative data – such as interviews with managers – that is usually presented as supplementary information.

One's philosophical perspective often plays a key role in choosing between qualitative and quantitative research methods. For instance, researchers who subscribe to interpretivism, which is closely associated with constructivism, deem that, unlike natural scientists seeking to explain nonintentional phenomena, the job of social scientists is to investigate intentional phenomena by interpreting the meanings attached to the phenomena by their actors (Schutz, 1970). Interpretivists generally adopt a socially constructed view of reality and a relativist stance such that "diverse meanings are assumed to exist and to influence how people understand and respond to the objective world" (Gephart, 2004, p. 457). Interpretivists aim to "interpret the meanings and actions of actors according to their own subjective frame of reference" (Williams, 2000, p. 210). Thus, social phenomena are meaningful in the sense that they are what they are according to the interpretation of the actors involved. The study of such phenomena often involves a "double hermeneutic" – researchers must interpret their subjects' interpretations because the latter's understanding and sensemaking are an integral part of the study (Danermark et al., 2002). The usual archival data, such as Compustat and Worldscope, can rarely capture such information; intensive interviews and observations are required to understand the phenomena. Hence, qualitative methods such as ethnographies and case studies are preferred to quantitative methods.

In contrast to interpretivism, positivism aims to discover law-like relationships among a set of empirically measurable constructs that have predictive power. Using statistical methods to analyze large datasets is a major way of developing a nomothetic body of knowledge. Since positivism relies on correlations between variables to identify empirical regularities and infer causal relations, reliability of results increases with sample size, other things being equal. Hence, positivist researchers tend to use quantitative methods, such as experiments, questionnaire surveys and analysis of archival data, in preference to qualitative methods. Yet a caveat is that positivists do not confine themselves to quantitative research.[5] For example, in political science, there is the term "qualitative positivist methodologies" (Falleti & Lynch, 2009). As Phillips (1987, p. 96) well says, "A positivist, *qua* positivist, is not committed to any particular research design. There is nothing in the doctrines of positivism that necessitates a love of statistics or distaste for case studies."

While most positivists are happy to test a theory using quantitative methods only, critical realists would object to such an approach. The issue is to do with the mechanisms mentioned above. In econometrics, a distinction is made between structural and reduced models (Johnston, 1991). The former contains formulas representing the relation of every dependent variable to its independent variables on various levels, while the latter displays the net or overall relation between the dependent variable and the ultimate independent variables. Expressed in the words of causation, reduced models connect the initial cause(s) and the ultimate effect of a causal chain (i.e., the two ends of the chain), whereas structural models also include at least some of the intermediate causes along the causal chain. As such, a causal mechanism is better represented by a structural model. Quantitative studies, especially those based on analysis of archival data, are mostly based on reduced models. From a critical realist perspective, a basic purpose of testing a theory is to investigate the extent to which its proposed mechanisms are consistent with events observed (Sayer, 1992). Since a reduced model only poorly represents the related causal mechanism, a quantitative study based on the model fails to rigorously test the mechanism and thus the theory in question (Tsang, 2006). The neglect of this weakness of quantitative studies led to Williamson's (1996, p. 55) erroneous claim that transaction cost economics "is an empirical success story," because most of the empirical tests of his theory had been based on reduced models, at least at the time of his claim.

Positivists and critical realists also have different evaluations of the same quantitative method. A good illustrative example is that critical realists generally consider structural equation modeling (SEM) a better method than various types of regression analysis. One key reason is that SEM enables in one shot analysis of a complicated model with mediators and moderators, such as Tsang's (2002) model of knowledge acquisition in the context of international joint ventures. Such a model can better represent the underlying mechanisms than regression analyses that are in the form of reduced models. Another reason is that scholars like Pearl (1998) have strengthened tremendously the causal foundation of SEM during the past two decades or so. Thus, SEM has become a more useful tool. In contrast, positivists are less receptive to SEM. Researchers use SEM to examine the relationships between latent variables and their measured indicators, as well as relationships among the latent variables. Yet positivists hold a position that opposes unobservable theoretical entities, such as the latent variables of SEM. This can be traced back to the Vienna Circle that created positivism. Moritz Schlick (1959), the founder of the Circle, rejected unobservable theoretical entities when he discussed the existence of electrons inside a nucleus. Critical realists, on the other hand, welcome the inclusion of latent variables because they "may be used to represent complex, multifaceted concepts that would otherwise be impossible to measure" (Pratschke, 2003, p. 23). Positivists are not just unimpressed but in fact deterred by SEM's so-called strength of causal inference, which is incompatible with their view that "cause," as a force or theoretical entity, cannot be observed or measured. According to the positivist principle of verification, statements that can't be verified have no content; causal statements are nonverifiable statements.

Unfortunately, many studies of macro management phenomena, such as strategy research, are based on reduced models, as indicated by studies published in *Strategic Management Journal*. Using a critical realist perspective, Kent Miller and I propose a four-step approach for advancing theory testing that prioritizes identifying and testing for the presence and effects of causal mechanisms hypothesized by a theory. The four steps are: (1) identifying the hypothesized mechanisms, (2) testing for the presence of the mechanisms in the empirical setting, (3) testing isolated causal relations using experimental or quasi-experimental designs, and (4) testing the theoretical system using correlational methods. In addition to the analysis of archival data, which is used in step 4, we include laboratory experiments, behavioral simulations, quasi-experiments, case studies, ethnography, and grounded theory building in field settings for the other three steps (Miller & Tsang, 2011). Our principle is that each research method has its own merits and demerits; a comprehensive test of a theory has to employ a variety of methods to exploit each method's merits.

INTERPRETATION OF RESEARCH RESULTS

A key objective of management research is to explain phenomena that have significant managerial implications. There are various ways of formulating explanations from empirical results (see Tsang, 2023 for a review). Philosophical perspectives affect not only which research methods are preferred but also how research results are interpreted for explanatory purposes. Management researchers are probably more aware of the former than the latter influence of philosophical perspectives because, say, constructivists and interpretivists obviously prefer qualitative methods, whereas the interpretation of, say, regression coefficients should not be affected by one's philosophical perspective. Here, I focus on two issues, (1) explanation versus prediction and (2) generalization, which are associated with quantitative and qualitative methods.

Hempel's (1965) covering-law model of explanation requires that acceptable answers to the question "Why did an event occur?" must offer information which shows that the event *is* to be expected under the same or very similar circumstances in which it occurred. Conversely, an adequate scientific prediction potentially offers an adequate scientific explanation for the occurrence of the event it predicts. In other words, there is a symmetry between explanation and prediction − every explanation is a potential prediction and every prediction is a potential explanation. This positivist view is sometimes reflected in statistics textbooks, a typical example being: "Knowing the intercept and the slope, we can predict Y for a given X value. For instance, if we encounter a Riverside city employee with ten years of schooling, then we would predict his or her income would be $12,398" (Lewis-Beck, 1980, p. 19). That is, a regression coefficient is interpreted as a tool for making predictions. Sometimes, prediction is even prioritized: "One use of MRC [multiple regression/correlation analysis] is for prediction, literally forecasting, with only incidental attention to explanation" (Cohen et al., 2003, p. 95).

The stress on the ability of statistical models to predict is reflected in this famous passage by Friedman (1953, pp. 14–15):

> Truly important and significant hypotheses will be found to have "assumptions" that are wildly inaccurate descriptive representations of reality, and, in general, the more significant the theory, the more unrealistic the assumptions ... the relevant question to ask about the "assumptions" of a theory is not whether they are descriptively "realistic," for they never are, but whether they are sufficiently good approximations for the purpose in hand. And this question can be answered by seeing whether the theory works, which means whether it yields sufficiently accurate predictions.

Friedman's instrumentalist view of theory was a response to the heated debate aroused by Lester's (1946) empirical study of US business executives who falsified marginal theory's assumption that business executives arrive at their production decisions through consulting schedules or multivariate functions showing marginal cost and marginal revenue. That is, Lester found that the explanation assumed by marginal theory was inconsistent with his result. Friedman's interpretation of Lester's result seems to be that marginal theory should not be abandoned solely because of the inconsistency and that the theory is acceptable so far as it can generate fairly accurate predictions.

In contrast to positivists and instrumentalists, critical realists focus on the explanatory, not predictive, power of a theory. As Kaplan (1964, p. 347) well says, "if we look at the explanations which actually occur in science as well as in everyday life, and not only at what an ideal explanation would be or what all explanations are 'in principle,' it appears that we often have explanations without being able to predict." Critical realists are not satisfied with a statistical model that merely generates accurate predictions based on covariational analyses. Rather, they attempt to specify discrete causal paths that connect the variables together (i.e., the underlying mechanism). As such, they would take Lester's result seriously because it shows that the mechanism proposed by marginal theory concerning how business executives arrive at their production decisions is inaccurate. Instead of trying to see whether the statistical model that produced the current results can predict accurately, they focus on examining how far the results are consistent with the mechanism proposed by the theory in question and what further tests are needed to investigate the mechanism.

The next issue is empirical generalization – whether the findings of a study are considered as typical of the population from which the sample was drawn or whether they are typical of another population (Tsang, 2014a). Generalization is a challenge that qualitative researchers often face because of the small-N problem (Steinmetz, 2004). Over 30 years ago, Bryman (1989, p. 172) stated that "the problem of generalization is often perceived as the chief drawback of case study research." This stigma associated with qualitative studies in general and case studies in particular persists. My discussion is based on case studies, which form the bulk of qualitative studies published in management journals.

Again, different philosophical perspectives have different interpretations of how generalizable case findings are. Interpretivists, who prefer qualitative methods, hold several different views on this matter. An extreme view simply denies generalization, as captured by Lincoln and Guba's (2000) eye-catching title "The Only Generalization Is: There Is No Generalization" of their paper. The core rationale is that multiple "realities" are created by different parties related to a phenomenon, and generalization glosses over such nuances. For instance, Denzin (1983) argues that every instance of human interaction represents "a slice from the life world" (p. 134) carrying various layers of meaning. Investigation of an instance of human interaction must be done hermeneutically and be regarded as carrying "its own logic, sense of order, structure, and meaning" (p. 134). As such, it makes little sense to interpret a studied instance of human interaction as being generalizable to other instances. A less extreme view is that case studies involve a special kind of generalization. Stake and Trumbull (1982), for example, create the term "naturalistic generalization," which describes a kind of interpretation by the reader of a case study concerning the similarities and differences between the case and a new setting that the reader encounters.

Positivists adopt statistical generalization as the method of generalizing research results. Since a case study is based on a very small sample, its contribution to establishing law-like relationships is marginal. Although positivism does not rule out case studies as a research method, it interprets case findings as having weak generalizability compared with the results of a normal quantitative study. Thus, case studies are necessarily exploratory in nature. For instance, Mohr (1985, p. 66) argues that the case study method "generally provides a better opportunity than large-sample research to hunt around for ideas and hypotheses in a new area – the exploratory-research function." Relationships identified in a case study have to be confirmed by allegedly more conclusive quantitative, large-N studies.

Critical realists are more sanguine than positivists about the generalizability of case findings, although they agree that it is not possible to statistically generalize case findings to the population from which the cases were drawn. Case studies enable researchers to explore the interaction of structures, events, human actions, and contexts for identifying and explicating mechanisms in a natural setting (Wynn & Williams, 2012). Compared with quantitative methods, case studies are better positioned to discover potential relations that are "causal, structural, and substantial, i.e., relations of connections" (Sayer, 1992, p. 246). Although the extent of regularities observed in the social world is smaller than that in the natural world, social phenomena are not completely chaotic. For example, with rare exceptions, cars stop when the traffic light turns red. Lawson (1997) describes this situation by coining the term "demi-regularity" – "a partial event regularity which prima facie indicates the occasional, but less than universal, actualization of a mechanism or tendency, over a definite region of time-space" (p. 204). The existence of demi-regularities in the social world implies that unless a study investigated cases that happened to be outliers, its findings often reflect certain typical features of the population from which the cases were drawn. Therefore, it is meaningful for researchers to make generalization claims based on the case findings, especially when the study consists of multiple and/or longitudinal cases (Tsang, 2014b).

TIPS FOR SELF-STUDYING PHILOSOPHY

Despite the intimate connection between philosophy and management research, my observation is that many, if not most, management scholars' knowledge of philosophy seldom extends beyond the philosophy of science seminar they took during their doctoral training (assuming that such a seminar was in the doctoral program concerned). Worse still, this meager knowledge dwindles with time. It is not difficult to spot errors from time to time when I read management papers that contain a significant philosophical element. For instance, Footnote 5 of Welch et al.'s (2011) article claims that Popper's falsificationism is a variant of positivism, and thus, the philosophical orientation of the natural-experiment approach is stated as "positivist (falsificationist)" in their Table 1. This is a factual error because Popper severely criticized positivism in his writings, for example: "Everybody knows nowadays that logical positivism is dead. But nobody seems to suspect that there may be a question to be asked here – the question 'Who is responsible?' or, rather, the question 'Who has done it?'...I fear that I must admit responsibility" (Popper, 2002, p. 99). Another example is Alvarez and Barney (2010) mistaking empiricism for critical realism (see Ramoglou, 2013 for the critique).

In this section, I share my experience of studying philosophy with those who are interested in enhancing their knowledge of the subject.[6] A pertinent question is: "Other than publishing philosophy-based articles in management journals (like I did), what are the benefits of learning philosophy?" Admittedly, the benefits are less tangible than those of, say, learning the methods of checking for endogeneity in a statistical model. In the context of this chapter, making an unconsciously held philosophical perspective explicit would enable management scholars to better understand the perspective so that they could use it consistently and productively in their research activities. For me, I enjoy the intellectual stimulation gained from reading philosophy, similar to the pleasure people usually gain from their hobbies. In addition to this abstract benefit, philosophy helps me formulate more rigorous arguments and spot more readily errors in others' arguments. When I worked with my coauthors Kai-man Kwan and John Williams, both professional philosophers, I noticed that they were much sharper than I in these aspects of theorizing. I believe their formal training in philosophy made the difference.

To start with, I have been asked occasionally by peers whether I studied philosophy in my undergraduate education. My somewhat surprising answer is a clear "no" because I didn't take any courses in philosophy during my undergraduate years. When I studied in the management doctoral program at the University of Cambridge, despite not registering formally, I took the late Peter Lipton's philosophy of science course in 1994. I admired his ability to show how profound philosophical concepts and arguments could be presented with little pedantic pretense. This is the style I attempt to emulate when I write articles with a significant philosophical element.[7] Lipton's course was the only formal training in philosophy I received and was one of the most enjoyable courses I have ever taken. My knowledge of philosophy came mostly from self-study; I have been reading about philosophy as a hobby since I was a teenager. My knowledge on the topic thus accumulated gradually and naturally over the years. Before providing some tips for learning philosophy, I would like to highlight two main obstacles.

Obstacles

First, as a subject, philosophy (or Western philosophy, to be specific) is much broader and has a much longer history than management. It consists of highly interrelated branches. To understand philosophy of science (and social science), which is one of the most relevant branches for management research, background knowledge of metaphysics and epistemology is required. To acquire the latter knowledge, it is necessary to gain some knowledge of the history of Western philosophy, at least since Socrates. Moreover, a basic understanding of logic is essential for understanding philosophical arguments. Since these arguments are expressed through language, some knowledge of philosophy of language will help a great deal.

Second, philosophical arguments are far more sophisticated and difficult to understand than their management counterparts. While this point should be obvious, unconvinced readers may try reading Popper's (1959) *The Logic of Scientific Discovery* and comparing it with Cyert and March's (1992) *A Behavioral Theory of the Firm*. Both books are landmark works, and all three scholars are highly respected in their respective fields. Management scholars may counter that this is not a fair comparison because they have received training that helps them understand the latter but not the former. Putting aside that factor, they can still appreciate the much greater extent of background knowledge and intellectual capability required for understanding the former. This was the feedback I received from a couple of peers. Moreover, it should be noted that Popper is one of the few great philosophers to be well known for lucid writing. There are several philosophers, such as Derrida, Hegel, Heidegger, Nietzsche, and Wittgenstein, whose works are hard to decipher.

Acquiring the Knowledge

The above two obstacles suggest that a huge investment of time and effort is needed to grasp a basic understanding of philosophy. For those who remain undeterred, I would suggest starting with Russell's (1912 [1997]) *The Problems of Philosophy*, which was published more than a century ago but remains as one of the best, if not the best, introductions to philosophy. Like Popper, Russell was a lucid writer. This short book was one of the first philosophy books I read decades ago. It begins with this question: "Is there any knowledge in the world which is so certain that no reasonable man could doubt it?" (p. 7). To answer that question, Russell challenges a commonsensical view: "I believe that, if any other normal person comes into my room, he will see the same chairs and tables and books and papers as I see, and that the table which I see is the same as the table which I feel pressing against my arm" (p. 8). Then, he picks the table as an example to show that our knowledge of it may not be as certain as we may have thought. His razor-sharp analysis of the experience of seeing and touching a table caused me to doubt seriously whether the table in front of me at the time of reading his book really existed! As a teenager, this was a life-changing experience for me intellectually because Russell's analysis was not the kind of argument found in subjects – such as history, geography, physics, chemistry, biology, and mathematics – that I took in school.

After reading *The Problems of Philosophy*, one should have a preliminary answer to the question: Is philosophy my cup of tea? If the answer is "yes," one may start reading the history of Western philosophy, such as Russell (1945) and Scruton (2002). The former is a general and rather brief introduction to the entire history of philosophy up to his time of writing while the latter focuses on more recent developments in philosophy. For very motivated readers, I recommend Soames' (2003a, 2003b) two-volume *Philosophical Analysis in the Twentieth Century* instead of Scruton's (2002) relatively brief text. Having gained some knowledge of philosophy, one may then like to focus on philosophy of science, the branch of philosophy more related to research methodology. A good starter is Chalmers's (2013) popular introduction *What Is This Thing Called Science?* Another easy-to-understand text is by Losee (2005), who discusses the testing, falsifying and replacing of scientific theories. More ambitious learners may proceed to the original works of Popper, Kuhn, Hempel, Carnap, Lakatos, Feyerabend, and so on. As to philosophy of social science, I recommend Fay (1996) as the starting point.

Like I did at Cambridge, management researchers may sit in philosophy courses offered at their universities. It is also fortunate that nowadays there are free lecture series on various branches of philosophy available via the Internet. I must admit, however, that my own learning journey has been lonely. To avoid a lonely experience, I would recommend the formation of study groups in which members set up a reading schedule, hold regular meetings, discuss selected texts, and question one another's understanding. Mutual support, both intellectual and emotional, can help sustain one's interest. Sitting in philosophy courses also provides a group learning environment, although one is more in control in a study group setting than in a course.

It is natural that one is unable to understand some of the arguments in a text, given the complexity of philosophical arguments. The resulting frustration is understandable, as arguments in the management literature are much simpler. Instead of giving up, though, one should put aside the puzzles and move on. My experience is that as I read more, I managed to make sense of what I could not understand previously. I was thrilled by such "Eureka!" moments. As mentioned, philosophy consists of highly interrelated branches. When one has accumulated more knowledge of these branches and started to connect the dots, one's comprehension will be enhanced.

Adopting a Philosophical Perspective

There are several popular philosophical perspectives among management researchers, such as positivism, empiricism, realism, constructivism, and interpretivism. One may like to select one perspective as the overarching guidance for one's research and then read more about that perspective. Years ago, I received this comment from a journal editor on my philosophy-based submission: "The choice of an ontological stand is necessarily subjective and guided by one's beliefs, so it is impossible to claim that one perspective is better reasoned than others." There is some truth in the first part of the comment, but not in the second; the comment reflects the editor's poor philosophical knowledge. The above example of Theranos shows that one perspective *can* be better than others. Russell (1945) shows how to evaluate a philosophical perspective. After describing a perspective, Russell often provides his critique in terms of how far the perspective is consistent logically (e.g., in his comment on Descartes), what loopholes the perspective contains (e.g., Kant), and/or whether the philosopher practiced what he preached (e.g., Schopenhauer). The following passage illustrates succinctly his sometimes bitter critique:

> John Stuart Mill, in his *Utilitarianism*, offers an argument which is so fallacious that it is hard to understand how he can have thought it valid. He says: Pleasure is the only thing desired; therefore pleasure is the only thing desirable. He argues that the only things visible are the only things seen, the only things audible are things heard, and similarly the only things desirable are things desired. He does not notice that a thing is "visible" if it *can* be seen, but "desirable" if it *ought* to be desired. Thus "desirable" is a word presupposing an ethical theory; we cannot infer what is desirable from what is desired. (p. 778)

Once a perspective is adopted, it should be applied consistently to one's research. Occasionally, I notice self-contradictions in this respect. For example, Chia (1996, 2003), who holds a radical postmodernist position, attaches the "science" label to management research and so creates the oxymoron "postmodern science." It is an oxymoron simply because scientific endeavors rely on confidence in the power of reason whereas the postmodernist movement can be described as "the counter-Enlightenment attack on reason" (Hicks, 2011, p. 23). Science generally subscribes to a realist ontology and an objectivist epistemology. In contrast, postmodernism adopts an anti-realist ontology and a socially subjectivist epistemology. Needless to say, blunders like Chia's should be avoided.

On a personal note, I adopt a more balanced reading approach, which has helped to sustain my interest in this long and sometimes frustrating learning journey. In addition to reading cold, hard analytic philosophy, I also benefit spiritually from continental philosophy and Chinese philosophy. In fact, existentialism − in particular, the writings of Albert Camus − partly shaped my character during my adolescent years. Decades later, the COVID-19 pandemic reminds me of the foresight of Camus's (1948) masterpiece *The Plague*. Socrates is a moral role model who I not only admire but also try to emulate. While I must admit that I am a poor student, I often remind myself of Socrates' renowned dictum "An unexamined life is not worth living."

NOTES

1. I prefer using the word "perspective" instead of "paradigm" because the latter term has been used indiscriminately by management researchers in a wide variety of ways – or, abused, to be precise. For instance, Mir and Watson (2000) use the terms "realist paradigm" and "industry structure paradigm." Obviously, these two meanings of "paradigm" are very different, and such usage of "paradigm" simply lacks academic rigor and gives rise to confusion. Many, if not most, management researchers are unaware that even Kuhn (1962), who brought the term to academia, failed to clearly define its meaning (Masterman, 1970).

2. Logical positivism should be distinguished from Auguste Comte's positivism from which the former originated. For instance, while Comte's positivism is "a rejection of any tenet that could not be empirically grounded" (Cashdollar, 2000, p. 218), logical positivism has a stronger antirealist stance concerning unobservable theoretical entities.

3. This is a highly simplistic presentation of Hume's profound and elegant argument. Interested readers may refer to Beebee's (2006) superb treatment of the topic.

4. The profitability requirement is for entrepreneurial opportunities in business. The corresponding requirement in social entrepreneurship depends on the nature of the social enterprise in question. For instance, if one comes up with a new way to motivate the residents of a community to send their children to school, the requirement could be an increase in the educational level of the community. Again, the opportunity has to result in a positive outcome; it just makes no sense for one to claim exploiting an opportunity that leads to a lower educational level in the community as the objective of setting up a social enterprise.

5. My observation is that some management researchers automatically associate quantitative research with positivism; that is, whenever they encounter a quantitative study, their knee-jerk reaction is that it is a piece of positivist-based research. This view is flawed in that other philosophical perspectives, such as realism, empiricism, and instrumentalism, also accommodate the principles of quantitative research.

6. These suggestions are based on a similar section of my article published in a Chinese journal (Tsang, 2021). The discussion here is more elaborate.

7. When I reviewed philosophy-based articles submitted to management journals, occasionally I noticed that authors, most of whom should be management researchers, used philosophical jargons with an implicit intention to scare off reviewers. In addition to showing off their philosophical knowledge, these authors' presumption seems to be that when reviewers can't understand the jargons, they will probably refrain from giving negative comments and a "rejection" recommendation; how can one criticize arguments that one doesn't have sufficient knowledge to understand? This is precisely a writing style I try to avoid.

REFERENCES

Alvarez, S. A., & Barney, J. B. (2010). Entrepreneurship and epistemology: The philosophical underpinnings of the study of entrepreneurial opportunities. *Academy of Management Annals*, 4, 557–583.

Alvarez, S. A., Barney, J. B., & Anderson, P. (2013). Forming and exploiting opportunities: The implications of discovery and creation processes for entrepreneurial and organizational research. *Organization Science*, 24(1), 301–317.

Ayers, M. R. (1968). *The refutation of determinism*. Methuen.

Beebee, H. (2006). *Hume on causation*. Routledge.

Benardete, S. (2006). *The being of the beautiful: Plato's Theaetetus, Sophist, and Statesman*. University of Chicago Press.

Berger, P. L., & Luckmann, T. (1967). *The social construction of reality*. Anchor Books.

Bhaskar, R. (1978). *A realist theory of science* (2nd ed.). Harvester Press.

Brown, A., Hecker, K. G., Bok, H., & Ellaway, R. H. (2021). Strange bedfellows: Exploring methodological intersections between realist inquiry and structural equation modeling. *Journal of Mixed Methods Research, 15*(4), 485–506.

Bryman, A. (1989). *Research methods and organization studies.* Unwin Hyman.

Camus, A. (1948). *The plague* (translated by S. Gilbert). Modern Library.

Carreyrou, J. (2020). *Bad blood: Secrets and lies in a Silicon Valley startup.* Vintage Books.

Cashdollar, C. D. (2000). Positivism. In G. B. Ferngren (Ed.), *The history of science and religion in the Western tradition* (pp. 216–222). Garland Publishing.

Chalmers, A. F. (2013). *What is this thing called science?* (4th ed.). University of Queensland Press.

Chia, R. (1996). The problem of reflexivity in organizational research: Towards a postmodern science of organization. *Organization, 3*(1), 31–59.

Chia, R. (2003). Organization theory as a postmodern science. In H. Tsoukas & C. Knudsen (Eds.), *The Oxford handbook of organization theory* (pp. 113–140). Oxford University Press.

Cohen, J., Cohen, P., West, S. G., & Aiken, L. S. (2003). *Applied multiple regression/correlation analysis for the behavioral sciences* (3rd ed.). Routledge.

Cyert, R. M., & March, J. G. (1992). *A behavioral theory of the firm* (2nd ed.). Blackwell.

Danermark, B., Ekström, M., Jakobsen, L., & Karlsson, J. C. (2002). *Explaining society: Critical realism in the social sciences.* Routledge.

Denzin, N. K. (1983). Interpretive interactionism. In G. Morgan (Ed.), *Beyond methods: Strategies for social research* (pp. 129–146). Sage.

Douglas, H. E. (2009). Reintroducing prediction to explanation. *Philosophy of Science, 76*(4), 444–463.

Falleti, T. G., & Lynch, J. F. (2009). Context and causal mechanisms in political analysis. *Comparative Political Studies, 42*(9), 1143–1166.

Fay, B. (1996). *Contemporary philosophy of social science.* Blackwell.

Friedman, M. (1953). *Essays in positive economics.* University of Chicago Press.

Gephart, R. P., Jr. (2004). Qualitative research and the *Academy of Management Journal. Academy of Management Journal, 47*(4), 454–462.

Harré, R. (1986). *Varieties of realism: A rationale for the natural sciences.* Basil Blackwell.

Hempel, C. G. (1965). *Aspects of scientific explanation.* Free Press.

Hicks, S. R. C. (2011). *Explaining postmodernism: Skepticism and socialism from Rousseau and Foucault* (Expanded ed.). Ockham's Razor Publishing.

Hume, D. (1999). *An enquiry concerning human understanding,* edited by T. L. Beauchamp. Oxford University Press.

Johnston, J. (1991). *Econometric methods* (3rd ed.). McGraw-Hill.

Kaplan, A. (1964). *The conduct of inquiry.* Chandler Publishing.

Kuhn, T. S. (1962). *The structure of scientific revolutions.* University of Chicago Press.

Lawson, T. (1997). *Economics and reality.* Routledge.

Lester, R. A. (1946). Shortcomings of marginal analysis for wage-employment problems. *American Economic Review, 36*(1), 63–82.

Lewis-Beck, M. S. (1980). *Applied regression.* Sage.

Lincoln, Y. S., & Guba, E. G. (2000). The only generalization is: There is no generalization. In R. Gomm, M. Hammersley & P. Foster (Eds.), *Case study: Key issues, key texts* (pp. 27–44). Sage.

Locke, J. (1996 [1689]). *An essay concerning human understanding,* abridged and edited by K. P. Winkler. Hackett Publishing.

Losee, J. (2005). *Theories on the scrap heap: Scientists and philosophers on the falsification, rejection, and replacement of theories.* University of Pittsburgh Press.

Machamer, P., Darden, L., & Craver, C. F. (2000). Thinking about mechanisms. *Philosophy of Science, 67*(1), 1–25.

Masterman, M. (1970). The nature of a paradigm. In I. Lakatos & A. Musgrave (Eds.), *Criticism and the growth of knowledge* (pp. 59–89). Cambridge University Press.

McMullen, J. S., Plummer, L. A., & Acs, Z. J. (2007). What is an entrepreneurial opportunity?. *Small Business Economics, 28*(4), 273–283.

Miller, K. D., & Tsang, E. W. K. (2011). Testing management theories: Critical realist philosophy and research methods. *Strategic Management Journal, 32*(2), 139–158.

Mir, R., & Watson, A. (2000). Strategic management and the philosophy of science: The case for a constructivist methodology. *Strategic Management Journal, 21*(9), 941–953.

Mohr, L. B. (1985). The reliability of the case study as a source of information. In R. F. Coulam & R. A. Smith (Eds.), *Advances in information processing in organizations* (Vol. 2, pp. 65–93). JAI Press.

Pearl, J. (1998). Graphs, causality, and structural equation models. *Sociological Methods & Research, 27*(2), 226–284.

Phillips, D. C. (1987). *Philosophy, science, and social inquiry: Contemporary methodological controversies in social science and related applied fields of research.* Pergamon Press.

Popper, K. (1959). *The logic of scientific discovery.* Harper & Row.

Popper, K. (2002). *Unended quest.* Routledge.

Pratschke, J. (2003). Realistic models? Critical realism and statistical models in the social sciences. *Philosophica, 71*(1), 13–38.

Ramoglou, S. (2013). On the misuse of realism in the study of entrepreneurship. *Academy of Management Review, 38*(3), 463–465.

Ramoglou, S., & Tsang, E. W. K. (2016). A realist perspective of entrepreneurship: Opportunities as propensities. *Academy of Management Review, 41*(3), 410–434.

Roy, I. (2021, February 17). Theranos – Silicon Valley's greatest startup disaster. *The Medium.* https://medium.com/thedarkside/theranos-silicon-valleys-greatest-startup-disaster-b2d3fbcf3154

Russell, B. (1912 [1997]). *The problems of philosophy.* Oxford University Press.

Russell, B. (1945). *A history of Western philosophy.* Simon & Schuster.

Sayer, A. (1992). *Method in social science* (2nd ed.). Routledge.

Schlick, M. (1959). Positivism and realism. In A. J. Ayer (Ed.), *Logical positivism* (pp. 82–107). Free Press.

Schutz, A. (1970). *On phenomenology and social relations.* University of Chicago Press.

Scruton, R. (2002). *A short history of modern philosophy: From Descartes to Wittgenstein* (2nd ed.). Routledge.

Shane, S., & Venkataraman, S. (2000). The promise of entrepreneurship as a field of research. *Academy of Management Review, 25*(1), 217–226.

Soames, S. (2003a). *Philosophical analysis in the twentieth century, Volume 1: The dawn of analysis.* Princeton University Press.

Soames, S. (2003b). *Philosophical analysis in the twentieth century, Volume 2: The age of meaning.* Princeton University Press.

Stake, R. E., & Trumbull, D. J. (1982). Naturalistic generalizations. *Review Journal of Philosophy and Social Science, 7*(1–2), 1–12.

Steinmetz, G. (2004). Odious comparisons: Incommensurability, the case study, and "small N's" in sociology. *Sociological Theory, 22*(3), 371–400.

Strauss, A., & Corbin, J. (1990). *Basics of qualitative research: Grounded theory procedures and techniques.* Sage.

Tsang, E. W. K. (2002). Acquiring knowledge by foreign partners from international joint ventures in a transition economy: Learning-by-doing and learning myopia. *Strategic Management Journal, 23*(9), 835–854.

Tsang, E. W. K. (2006). Behavioral assumptions and theory development: The case of transaction cost economics. *Strategic Management Journal, 27*(11), 999–1011.

Tsang, E. W. K. (2014a). Case studies and generalization in information systems research: A critical realist perspective. *Journal of Strategic Information Systems, 23*(2), 174–186.

Tsang, E. W. K. (2014b). Generalizing from research findings: The merits of case studies. *International Journal of Management Reviews, 16*(4), 369–383.

Tsang, E. W. K. (2017). *The philosophy of management research.* Routledge.

Tsang, E. W. K. (2021). Why philosophy can help management research. *Quarterly Journal of Management,* (4), 8–22. (in Chinese).

Tsang, E. W. K. (2023). *Explaining management phenomena: A philosophical treatise.* Cambridge University Press.

Van Fraassen, B. C. (2008). *The empirical stance.* Yale University Press.

Welch, C., Piekkari, R., Plakoyiannaki, E., & Paavilainen-Mäntymäki, E. (2011). Theorising from case studies: Towards a pluralist future for international business research. *Journal of International Business Studies, 42*(5), 740–762.

Williams, M. (2000). Interpretivism and generalisation. *Sociology, 34*(2), 209–224.

Williamson, O. E. (1996). Economic organization: The case for candor. *Academy of Management Review, 21*(1), 48–57.

Wittgenstein, L. (1958). *Philosophical investigations*. Basil Blackwell.

Wood, M. S., & McKinley, W. (2010). The production of entrepreneurial opportunity: A constructivist perspective. *Strategic Entrepreneurship Journal, 4*(1), 66–84.

Wynn, D., Jr., & Williams, C. K. (2012). Principles for conducting critical realist case study research in information systems. *MIS Quarterly, 36*(3), 787–810.

THE SMART TOOL: ENCOURAGING STANDARDIZED AND REPLICABLE RESEARCH IN MANAGEMENT TO ENHANCE CREDIBILITY

Andrew B. Blake[a], Oleg V. Petrenko[b], Timothy J. Quigley[c], Aaron D. Hill[d] and Amrit Panda[a]

[a]Texas Tech University Rawls College of Business, USA
[b]University of Arkansas, USA
[c]University of Georgia, USA
[d]University of Florida, USA

ABSTRACT

Strategic management research faces increasing calls concerning our work's relevance, reliability and credibility. Management journals have addressed these concerns by elevating the expectations for scholars during the publication process, such as publishing code, scripts and data. While the authors' believe these changes are necessary for the field's long-term success, in the short term, there is a high resource cost for researchers (many with temporal constraints) to adjust to these new expectations. In this paper, the authors aim to decrease this cost on Strategic Management researchers in two ways. First, the authors discuss the vision, strengths and step-by-step instructions for the emerging code-sharing instrument – The SMART tool (Standardized Measures that are Accurate, Replicable and Time-saving, available at http://www.smartdata-tool.net/) – for Strategic Management research. Second, the authors discuss some essential conditions for the tool's benefits to be fully realized by the field. Together, this paper offers the initial steps for creating a collaborative and open-source ecosystem for code and data in Strategic Management research that can strengthen stakeholder confidence in the field.

Delving Deep
Research Methodology in Strategy and Management, Volume 15, 43–55
Copyright © 2025 Andrew B. Blake, Oleg V. Petrenko, Timothy J. Quigley, Aaron D. Hill and Amrit Panda
Published under exclusive licence by Emerald Publishing Limited
ISSN: 1479-8387/doi:10.1108/S1479-838720240000015003

Keywords: Replication; empirical generalization; code sharing; strategic management; open science; data reliability

INTRODUCTION

Scholars have called for shifts in practices to increase the openness and transparency of research (Aguinis et al., 2018; Mirowski, 2018; Schwab & Starbuck, 2017), such as encouraging or even requiring the publishing of code or scripts and data (Aytug et al., 2012; Banks et al., 2016; Freese, 2007; Nuijten et al., 2016), mandating preregistration of studies (Nosek et al., 2018) and embracing replication of prior work (Ethiraj et al., 2016). In straightforward terms, journals expect more from scholars during the publication process to ensure that the findings in published work are credible. To facilitate a smoother adjustment to these new expectations, we propose a response with the introduction of the SMART tool (Standardized Measures that are Accurate, Replicable and Time-saving; Quigley et al., 2023).

The SMART tool functions both as an archival data collection utility and a catalyst for a new ecosystem of open-source collaboration for management scholars. Specifically, the SMART tool allows users the capability to routinely collect, link and compute standardized firm-level variables across a spectrum of archival datasets offered by the Wharton Research Data Services (WRDS) – or what we refer to as "structuration code" that creates data. The tool is supported by an open-source website and library that enables scholars to (1) capture the formula and code for each variable offered by the SMART tool, (2) request additional variables to be added to the tool, (3) provide variable and code information for a specific variable, (4) request or provide data patches to known issues within the WRDS archival datasets and (5) validate current computations of standardized variables. We hope the functionality delivered by the SMART tool will foster a different mindset for archival data management that helps to change the culture of strategic management research.

This manuscript aims to facilitate the dissemination and use of the SMART tool. To do so, we first introduce the basis for the SMART tool, the overall vision for the ecosystem and the broader benefits the SMART tool can bring to the field of management. Second, we identify the strengths of the SMART tool and offer specific details on how to access and use it. Third, we highlight an essential condition for the success of the tool – an engaged and committed community of scholars and how scholars can contribute to this project to harness growing interest in creating an ecosystem that enhances the reliability and validity of our data and subsequent research.

THE SMART TOOL

The SMART tool is a free online resource that exemplifies the ideals we outline above and enables researchers to streamline the three-part database preparation process by offering (1) standardized code that automatically downloads and links

WRDS datasets; (2) a centralized catalog of popular indicators in the field of management, which includes exact definitions and mathematical formulas for each indicator; and (3) standardized code that can be executed using the open source statistical software R to automatically compute indicators that can be saved in R or exported to other formats (such as STATA, SAS or CSV). This code can be reproduced anytime, saved, reused in the future and modified or extended for more advanced or novel uses.

Before we engage in a detailed discussion, we first note our vision for this tool. What we present now is not a destination but rather a step in a journey toward credible and reproducible research practices in the field of strategic management. Our vision is that this tool becomes a community project where anyone can contribute to developing open-source code that is free to use for other researchers. From the start, we propose mechanisms for the maintenance and development of this tool by the community of interested researchers. While the code will be housed within the author team's control, anyone can submit additions and improvements to the tool to ensure its accuracy and effectiveness in promoting research. Such collaboration is a crucial purpose of GitHub. Alternatively, the existing repository can be duplicated and extended independently of the author team using GitHub's "fork" functionality.

One example of this approach would be the indicator list included in the tool. To come up with the initial indicator list for the first release version, the author team looked through three years of *Journal of Management* (*JOM*) and *Strategic Management Journal* (*SMJ*) and recorded every variable used in the empirical articles. Next, we analyzed one year of the *Academy of Management Journal, Organization Science* and *Administrative Science Quarterly* to record additional variables used in strategic management research not captured in our reviews of *JOM* and *SMJ*. A few additional variables were added, giving us the confidence that we had developed a comprehensive list of the most commonly used measures. In the following step, we identified variables that appeared more than three times in the articles yielding a list of 17 variables (some with varying specifications). These variables are the initial set of indicators included in the tool. We expect this set to grow as more people submit their variables (with definitions and formulas) to grow the tool and its effectiveness.

In what follows, we briefly highlight the various benefits of the SMART tool while pointing readers to more thorough discussions elsewhere before directing scholars to a free online tool, providing a guide and concluding with future research.

Standardized Measurement

Standardized measurement calculation and labeling have long been critical to systematic knowledge accumulation. For example, Block (1995) highlighted the long history of jingle and jangle fallacies and associated problems; the notion of "the jingle fallacy" – where two things are quantifiably different but labeled the same – dates back at least a century (Thorndike, 1904, p. 11) while the "jangle fallacy" – where things that are the quantifiably the same but labeled differently –

has been discussed nearly as long (Kelley, 1927, p. 64). This is not to say that different ways to calculate a measure are problematic – in contrast, different measures may be needed as scholars test novel theories or employ different methods. Further, different measures can enhance robustness, as in the multitrait–multimethod approach. Nonetheless, we still need to know what the measures are exactly and label them consistently for reference (Campbell & Fiske, 1959). To illustrate Hopkins & Lazonick (2016) showed how Execucomp includes multiple calculations of total executive compensation and that relationships and associated conclusions drawn can vary drastically across the different measures (i.e. which of the measures is used). Thankfully, Execucomp offers unique labels to differentiate among the measures of total executive compensation (e.g. see TDC1, TDC2, TOTAL_ALT1 and TOTAL_ALT2 in Execucomp variable descriptions), thus allowing clarity concerning exact calculation and concordant labeling.

The SMART tool offers an avenue to avoid both jingle and jangle fallacies. First, we provide exact definitions for each calculated or downloaded indicator. We include both written definitions and mathematical equations (calculated using the exact names of the variables downloaded from source datasets). Second, we allow users to use some indicators with alternative specifications (each with exact definitions). For example, Version 1.0 of the tool allows researchers to calculate multiple measures in multiple ways, with an example being return on assets (ROA) measured using three different definitions found in existing studies: (1) net income divided by total assets of a firm in a given fiscal year (ROA1); (2) net income of a given fiscal year divided by the average total assets of focal year t and prior year $t - 1$ (ROA2) and (3) earnings before interest divided by total assets in given fiscal year (ROA3). By standardizing measurement terminology and calculation, we ensure that quantifiably different measures are calculated consistently and labeled in a way that differentiates them, while identical measures are always calculated and labeled the same way.

Accurate

Beyond providing standardized measurement and terminology to aid clarity in measure explanation, the SMART tool improves measurement accuracy by helping avoid both unintentional errors and intentional manipulation in measurement calculation. Specifically, unintentional and intentional measurement inaccuracies occur for many reasons (Banks et al., 2016). By using calculations that are displayed publicly and have been checked for accuracy, the SMART tool avoids unintentional errors tied to human fallibility (e.g. a typographical error in a calculation). At the same time, the public nature of the SMART tool aids the comparison of means and standard deviations of data reported in a study, thus enabling inaccuracies to be caught during the review process. As such, intentional inaccuracies whereby scholars knowingly alter measures (e.g. to generate desired results) are more likely to be identified in the review process as well.

Relatedly, the SMART tool can facilitate more accurate findings. Based on the abovementioned executive total compensation example, Hopkins and Lazonick (2016) note how executives may be seen as making more or making less based on the measure used. Similar inconsistencies are noted in other common measures and shown to affect results (Lubatkin et al., 1993; Shinkle, 2012; Tan & Peng, 2003). Providing multiple, accurate measures can thus facilitate testing across measures and, thereby, offers an avenue to more accurate conclusions (Campbell & Fiske, 1959).

Replicable

The SMART tool can also facilitate replicable studies. For example, just as noting that total executive compensation was measured using TDC1 vs TDC2 or that ROA was captured using ROA1, ROA2 or ROA3, specificity with respect to what was measured can help those interested in replications follow the processes more closely. Rather than a generic statement about capturing total compensation or ROA, authors can refer to the variable names and calculations from the SMART tool, which, in turn, will enhance transparency and enable more accurate replication. Even with the best efforts of authors and reviewers to establish clarity, specific measures can be difficult to explain (Bergh et al., 2017). Pointing to a specific measure with consistent labeling, adding transparency regarding the mathematical formula and providing the exact code used in the computation can create this needed clarity. Old files may also be misplaced over time, so the precise labeling afforded by the SMART tool – much like stating the use of TDC1 or TDC2 – can assist in replicating prior data.

Time-Saving

On a practical level, the process of sourcing and matching data and subsequently calculating measures can be time intensive – and, while necessary – not particularly value-added for science. The SMART tool will free up valuable time and, thus, may spawn additional value creation by allowing scholars to pursue opportunities that are otherwise forsaken for want of time. In short, it might be better suited for scholars to focus their valuable, rare, inimitable and non-substitutable resource of time in other ways (Barney, 1991).

The SMART tool and associated time saving may beget related benefits as well. One is that the tool may be particularly helpful in alerting aspiring scholars to the many extant measures used in the field. Another is that the time-saving may promote better science by encouraging scholars to conduct additional tests. That is, we foresee that these data tool, especially as it expands, will help make scholars aware of multiple alternative measures (e.g. ROA1 and ROA2) and thus facilitate using the alternative measures to explore robustness or boundaries. At the same time, reviewers, knowing the ease of the SMART tool, may be more willing to ask for such tests. The time savings may render fewer desires to "cut corners" as well, further improving accuracies. Together, the results may be more accurate and give way to more replicable knowledge.

THE SMART TOOL INTERFACE

The SMART Tool is available at www.smartdatatool.net. The website includes a general description of the tool, detailed definitions and formulas for every indicator, instructions on how to use the tool and the actual tool that allows researchers to generate and download code. An important note is that the tool can access WRDS only if the user has an active subscription to the datasets. Therefore, researchers must enter their credentials that permit access to the data sources based on their active subscription. Security and privacy are key aspects of our tool; we do not store the credentials in any form. Instead, when users execute the code on their own computers, they are interactively prompted to enter their WRDS credentials to gain access to their subscribed datasets. The SMART tool, running on the user's computer, then connects to the WRDS server without ever storing or transferring user credentials outside the verification that occurs with WRDS.

We also recognize that no single preferred statistical tool exists for all scholars. To accommodate this, users can specify saving resulting data files in R, Stata, SPSS, SAS or CSV formats. The step-by-step instructions offered below also include visual representations that can be found on our website here: https://github.com/abblake/START/blob/main/Walkthrough.docx.

Step-by-step Instructions

While our vision for the SMART tool is to facilitate the ease with which scholars can collect and structure archival data reliably, there is an initial learning curve with getting started using the SMART tool, which includes appropriately installing and becoming familiar with the R and RStudio interface. This learning curve is balanced by the strengths of the SMART tool, which include reliability in linking separate datasets, mapping variable computational code to its mathematical formula and providing a platform to foster a vibrant community of scholars that actively contribute to idea generation, code sharing, data patches and additional data. Thus, the goal of this section is to thoroughly describe how one can overcome the initial learning curve and, at the same time, fully utilize the power of the SMART tool and its growing ecosystem.

Step 1: Installing R. The SMART tool is entirely composed in the software language R (www.r-project.org), an open-source statistical software. To install R for the first time, navigate to the website www.r-project.org and click on the CRAN link. Click on the 0-Cloud link to be directed to the website that enables you to download R. There will be a "Download and Install R" cell on this website. Select your operating system (i.e., Windows or Mac). *For Windows*, use the "base" link. *For Mac*, we suggest using the most up-to-date version listed. Once this file is downloaded, run the file and follow the installation instructions. You do not need to create a desktop link to R or have it visible to you, as you will be installing additional software, RStudio, that operates R in the background.

Step 2: Installing RStudio. Once R is fully installed, navigate to https://www.rstudio.com/ to download RStudio. RStudio is an integrated development environment, or put another way, an enhanced user interface for R that reduces the learning curve of R and offers additional features to maximize the versatility and power of R. To install RStudio, navigate to https://www.rstudio.com/, select Products from the main menu. A sub-menu will appear. Click on "Open Source." Another sub-menu will appear that shows R-Studio. Click the RStudio to continue. Click on the "Download RStudio Desktop" link on this page. The webpage will redirect to four versions of RStudio, and we suggest downloading the free version for now. Like R, you must select your operating system to continue downloading the file. Scroll down to the RStudio desktop. Next, run the downloaded install file and follow the onscreen instructions. Once the RStudio installation finishes, you are ready to familiarize yourself with RStudio.

Step 3: Familiarize yourself with R and RStudio. At first blush, the RStudio interface may seem complex. First, it is essential to review the basics of R. R is like other statistical languages used in management, such as SPSS and Stata, in that it is an interpretive computer language. An interpretive computer language allows users to write and use code in the same process rather than compiling that code into a piece of software. However, R differs from these two languages in a very distinct way. It is object-oriented. An object-oriented language actively stores into memory things like datasets and results to be recalled later by using a name assigned by the user. This R feature is extremely useful for structuring archival data. Multiple datasets can be recalled within a single iteration of R. When downloading datasets from WRDS, the SMART tool will automatically create object datasets to be later used for export.

RStudio leverages this language to empower the original R interface. Once RStudio is open, click File, New File and R script. You will now see four cells, each with its distinct purpose. It is vital to understand the function of each cell to run the SMART tool effectively. The top left cell is called the Source. This cell will display any file that R can open. You have opened an untitled R script for the SMART tool, which will house the R code produced by the SMART tool. For now, let us review the other cells. On the bottom left cell is the Console. The Console cell displays the code run by R and any errors in running the code. The Console is also helpful in running simple test code for something as simple as "1+1" or something more complex such as loading data into the R environment. The environment window (which includes history, connections and tutorial) is in the upper right. We will only focus on an explanation of the environment for the purposes of using the SMART tool.

The environment cell window displays and allows access to all objects loaded into R from either the Console or the Source cells. In the lower right, the final cell holds the Files, Plots, Packages, Help and Viewer panes. The Files pane enables users to load data from a specific folder. The Plots pane is where all plots generated from R are stored for viewing. The Packages pane shows all installed libraries (plug-ins) and the currently loaded libraries. The Viewer pane is where more complex visualizations are displayed. For the use of the SMART tool, the most important will be the packages tab, which enables users to review all the libraries loaded, as there are various requirements for the SMART tool to be run properly. Now you should be able to use the SMART Tool. Let us use the example below to understand how to launch and use the tool.

Step 4: Using the SMART tool. To maximize the utility of the SMART tool, it is best to introduce a basic use-case example. For instance, for the initial start of a paper, say we need to collect both ROA and CEO gender from Compustat and Execucomp, respectively. Navigate to www.smartdatatool.net and click the "Take me to the tool" link. Here, a new page will open. Because there are multiple measures of ROA offered identified from studies, as noted earlier, we will collect all three variables by clicking the check box labeled ROA1, ROA2 and ROA3 (definitions housed on the SMART tool website). We will also click the CEO Gender box under the "Variable Select:" list. Then, we will click the "Generate Code" link to the right to receive the code entered into our untitled R script. We then copy the generated code inside the grey box on the website and paste it into the untitled R script found in our instance of RStudio. Now that the code is in RStudio, we enter "CTRL+A" for Windows and then CTRL+Enter. For Macs, CMD+A and then CMD+Enter. RStudio will begin to process the SMART tool code, and we will receive several pop-up windows that request key information to tell RStudio. These requests include the directory where we want the data stored, the name of the data file, how we want it saved (e.g. Excel, SPSS and Stata), the start and end year of your data and finally, our WRDS credentials.

After R processes the code (typically takes several minutes), a dataset is created in the directory we specified to use in our analysis. Now you have a dataset that can be used for analytical models. Next, we offer a few observations that help highlight the tool's potential.

STRENGTHS AND OPPORTUNITIES

Understanding how variables are computed. An essential part of strategic management research is learning to compute key financial variables for our models. The challenge many of us face as aspiring and established scholars is the fact that there are various ways to compute the same variables. The SMART tool simplifies this challenge by creating a virtual library of variables and their mathematical formulas that are freely open to review. Circling back to our original example of ROA, using the SMART tool, we computed ROA1, ROA2 and ROA3 for our data analysis; yet, if one is new to R programing language, the formula from the code can seem complex. Navigating to www.smartdatatool.net and clicking "Formulas and Equations," each variable (such as ROA1, ROA2 and ROA3) is a reviewable mathematical formula that also includes a formalized definition of the variable. Overall, this takes the guesswork out of variable selection. Because now, formulas and code can be reviewed by the public and adjusted if needed. Another important strength of using the SMART tool to create datasets is that it allows them to be replicated precisely (because the code and specifications are known) by anyone at any time.

Community feedback. Strategic management as a field of study draws its energy from a community of scholars interested in advancing firm performance and behavior knowledge. While some strides are being made to create a community to share ideas and facilitate the growth of our field, we are still heavily reliant on analog discussions at conferences (official and unofficial) to exchange critical information and feedback about a particular source of data, measure, or method of collection. The SMART tool addresses this gap in knowledge transference. Specifically, it includes ways for others to provide feedback about a variable computation, request new variables and provide data patches about issues in an archival dataset or externally collected data. This feature can be accessed by navigating to www.smartdatatool.net, clicking community input and resources and then GitHub Collaboration. Here, all the code used in the SMART tool is public and reviewable. Users can click the "Issues" tab to post about a specific variable or request a new variable. Additionally, users can navigate to the "Discussions" page to introduce a new discussion or add to ongoing discussions about the SMART tool, a data patch or other ideas to foster growth in the community.

Building an Open-Source Ecosystem

Why Give Up Our Competitive Advantage?

Throughout the development of the SMART tool, analog discussions initiated by the authors to members of the strategic management community about the tool and its potential to foster growth in the field have been met with skepticism and excitement. The common thread emerging from these discussions dividing excitement from skepticism is a sense of losing a competitive advantage among community members when one shares code, data patches and external data. It is essential to address this upfront and clarify that a sense of losing a competitive advantage is likely overblown. First, simplifying data structuring routines developed in isolation is one fundamental driver for developing the SMART tool and open-source ecosystem. When scholars share their routines on variable creation (common or unique), there is one less intellectual barrier for others to leap over, making it easier for scholars inside and outside the field of strategy to review, understand and test the crucial insights revealed by a manuscript. It is not common that measuring a variable itself or combining data from widely available datasets will form a competitive advantage for a scholar. However, by removing the veil through code sharing for a measure or data combination, scholars increase the chances that their papers have a greater number of citations and strategic management scholarship's impact on the broader community.

Second, discussed in the literature and during Ph.D. seminars is the unsettling fact that some of the data we commonly use from archival sources include inaccuracies – common ones being that a non-trivial number of firms issues financial restatements and the removal of variables such as race and/or ethnicity in light of conceptualization concerns (e.g. BoardEx, 2021). These inaccuracies could be biasing our findings and our subsequent inferences. However, we have done little to resolve these known issues as a community. At the same time, grapevine discussions in the community indicate that some strategic management scholars consistently invest their time in correcting or patching inaccuracies they find in the data. In fact, some of the authors of this manuscript patched known errors in the RiskMetrics/ISS dataset, which is available in the SMART tool. Others sharing their patches, while likely heavily investing in these corrections, can facilitate the reliability of the data used in strategic management and increase the likelihood that their findings can be reproduced and cited.

Third, while common in social sciences, the strategic management community appears reluctant to share externally collected data. Some scholars are aware of this and actively incentivize sharing novel data (such as "data papers" that are now accepted in *SMJ*; Ethiraj et al., 2017). Admittedly, extensive time and financial resources will likely be invested in collecting external data, providing a semi-sustained competitive advantage in the publication process. Once scholars have leveraged their externally collected data, the competitive advantage of keeping the data private diminishes. However, scholars can facilitate the dissemination of their inferences from this external data (hopefully published) by sharing their data and allowing others to test their ideas and build from their theoretical contributions.

Taking all three points together, perhaps in the short term, scholars may be concerned with losing competitive advantage, particularly in cases of externally collected data. However, the long-term legitimacy of strategic management as a field must rely on the reliability of our data (Bergh et al., 2017), scholarly impact and community dissemination of knowledge to sustain a competitive advantage for the field of strategic management in the changing educational environment.

A Call to Senior Faculty in Particular

Our vision of the SMART tool and corresponding community will require contributions from aspiring, new and seasoned scholars. However, we believe the primary responsibility lies in the hands of the seasoned, tenured faculty, who likely have the resources in terms of time, data and available code to share. They also do not face the same challenges associated with a tenure clock and related view of a need to maintain a competitive advantage to be promoted from the assistant professor ranks, having already navigated the process. Thus, we call upon seasoned, tenured scholars, in particular, to share ideas, their code, data, data patches and the SMART tool with the broader strategic management community. Below, we provide some basic steps on how one interested can contribute and some ideas on disseminating the SMART tool.

Contributing to the SMART Tool

Sharing code. When one would like to share code to new versions of the SMART tool, they should navigate to www.smartdatatool.net and click community input and resources and then GitHub Collaboration. The web browser will take you to the community GitHub page. On the top of the page, there will be an "Issues" link. Click this link. Here, a list of upcoming additions to the SMART tool is listed, where someone can request their code to be added to the SMART tool. On the right-hand side, above the listed threads, there is a "New issue" button in green. Click this link and sign into your GitHub account. The GitHub account is free and takes just a few moments to register. Once the account is registered, add a title to the thread, press "CTRL+E" and paste your code into the new issue thread. Alternatively, you may drag and drop files into the "Leave a comment" box. Finally, there is a labels option on the right-hand side where the code is placed. Click the gear icon to label your thread a "code add request." Then hit "Submit new issue." The author team will review the posted code. Once approved, the authors will add you to the next iteration of the SMART tool.

Sharing data and data patches. This will follow the exact instructions until after entering the thread's title. First, click the "Attach files by dragging [. . .]" button directly underneath the "Leave a comment" section. This button allows users to upload data (a patch or dataset). After uploading the dataset, select the appropriate label (data patch or dataset) and click "Submit new issue."

Disseminating the SMART tool to others by corresponding with the community. There are several essential ways in which senior scholars can contribute to the SMART tool beyond sharing code, data or data patches. First, the SMART tool can be included in doctoral seminars either in a pure methods course or a specific course on strategic management. This inclusion helps to acquaint Ph.D. students with R and RStudio, which is becoming increasingly popular in management research. Also, it hastens the demystification process of structuring archival data commonly used in strategy research. Second, editors and reviewers should use the SMART tool to quickly reproduce data from submitted journal articles they are reviewing. This process can quickly reproduce common data points in a study, enabling reviewers to examine correlation tables and other critical aspects of the data. Third, they can use the SMART tool in their papers to showcase the benefits of transparent data collection and standardization for available variables. This action brings awareness to the powerful benefits of the SMART tool. Finally, we hope this article serves as a model for others, and scholars can continue with the general thrust we propose by building other tools that help the field.

CONCLUSION

Philosophically, the social science community is shifting towards a transparency-based approach to collecting and analyzing data. In this paper, we offer an approach that can help scholars cope with this change while simultaneously enhancing the legitimacy and growth of the community. Specifically, we introduce the SMART tool that helps to automate the process by creating publicly available, reproducible code to structure, compute and patch archival data common to the strategic management literature. This tool also establishes a foundational community where scholars can share ideas, code, external data and data patches that can facilitate the legitimization and growth of the field.

REFERENCES

Aguinis, H., Ramani, R. S., & Alabduljader, N. (2018). What you see is what you get? Enhancing methodological transparency in management research. *The Academy of Management Annals, 12*(1), 83–110. https://doi.org/10.5465/annals.2016.0011

Aytug, Z. G., Rothstein, H. R., Zhou, W., & Kern, M. C. (2012). Revealed or concealed? Transparency of procedures, decisions, and judgment calls in meta-analyses. *Organizational Research Methods, 15*(1), 103–133. https://doi.org/10.1177/1094428111403495

Banks, G. C., Rogelberg, S. G., Woznyj, H. M., Landis, R. S., & Rupp, D. E. (2016). Editorial: Evidence on questionable research practices: The good, the bad, and the ugly. *Journal of Business and Psychology, 31*(3), 323–338. https://doi.org/10.1007/s10869-016-9456-7

Barney, J. (1991). Firm resources and sustained competitive advantage. *Journal of Management, 17*(1), 99–120. https://doi.org/10.1177/014920639101700108

Bergh, D. D., Sharp, B. M., Aguinis, H., & Li, M. (2017). Is there a credibility crisis in strategic management research? Evidence on the reproducibility of study findings. *Strategic Organization, 15*(3), 423–436. https://doi.org/10.1177/1476127017701076

Block, J. (1995). A contrarian view of the five-factor approach to personality description. *Psychological Bulletin, 117*(2), 187–215. https://doi.org/10.1037/0033-2909.117.2.187

BoardEx. (2021). *Website discussion of variables.* https://www.boardex.com/diversity/. Accessed on January 31, 2023.

Campbell, D. T., & Fiske, D. W. (1959). Convergent and discriminant validation by the multitrait-multimethod matrix. *Psychological Bulletin, 56*(2), 81–105. https://doi.org/10.1037/h0046016

Ethiraj, S. K., Gambardella, A., & Helfat, C. E. (2016). Replication in strategic management: Replication in strategic management. *Strategic Management Journal, 37*(11), 2191–2192. https://doi.org/10.1002/smj.2581

Ethiraj, S. K., Gambardella, A., & Helfat, C. E. (2017). Improving data availability: A new SMJ initiative: Editorial. *Strategic Management Journal, 38*(11), 2145–2146. https://doi.org/10.1002/smj.2690

Freese, J. (2007). Replication standards for quantitative social science: Why not sociology? *Sociological Methods & Research, 36*(2), 153–172. https://doi.org/10.1177/0049124107306659

Hopkins, M., & Lazonick, W. (2016). *The mismeasure of Mammon: Uses and abuses of executive pay data.* SSRN Scholarly Paper No. 2877980. https://doi.org/10.2139/ssrn.2877980

Kelley, T. L. (1927). *Interpretation of educational measurements.* World Book.

Lubatkin, M., Merchant, H., & Srinivasan, N. (1993). Construct validity of some unweighted product-count diversification measures. *Strategic Management Journal, 14*(6), 433–449. https://doi.org/10.1002/smj.4250140604

Mirowski, P. (2018). The future(s) of open science. *Social Studies of Science, 48*(2), 171–203. https://doi.org/10.1177/0306312718772086

Nosek, B. A., Ebersole, C. R., DeHaven, A. C., & Mellor, D. T. (2018). The preregistration revolution. *Proceedings of the National Academy of Sciences, 115*(11), 2600–2606. https://doi.org/10.1073/pnas.1708274114

Nuijten, M. B., Hartgerink, C. H. J., van Assen, M. A. L. M., Epskamp, S., & Wicherts, J. M. (2016). The prevalence of statistical reporting errors in psychology (1985–2013). *Behavior Research Methods, 48*(4), 1205–1226. https://doi.org/10.3758/s13428-015-0664-2

Quigley, T. J., Hill, A. D., Blake, A., & Petrenko, O. (2023). Improving our field through code and data sharing. *Journal of Management, 49*(3), 875–880. https://doi.org/10.1177/01492063221141861

Schwab, A., & Starbuck, W. H. (2017). A call for openness in research reporting: How to turn covert practices into helpful tools. *The Academy of Management Learning and Education, 16*(1), 125–141. https://doi.org/10.5465/amle.2016.0039

Shinkle, G. A. (2012). Organizational aspirations, reference points, and goals: Building on the past and aiming for the future. *Journal of Management*, *38*(1), 415–455. https://doi.org/10.1177/0149206311419856

Tan, J., & Peng, M. W. (2003). Organizational slack and firm performance during economic transitions: Two studies from an emerging economy. *Strategic Management Journal*, *24*(13), 1249–1263. https://doi.org/10.1002/smj.351

Thorndike, E. L. (1904). *An introduction to the theory of mental and social measurements*. The Science Press.

HOW TO CROSS THE UNCANNY VALLEY: DEVELOPING MANAGEMENT LABORATORY STUDIES USING VIRTUAL REALITY

Timothy D. Hubbard and Michael Villano

University of Notre Dame, USA

ABSTRACT

Virtual reality (VR) presents an important technological advancement that can enable management researchers to improve their laboratory work and test theories previously considered untestable. VR places a participant in a virtual environment completely designed and controlled by the research team. These environments can range from anything as benign as a regular corporate board meeting or a job interview to as hostile as a CEO answering questions in front of Congress or witnessing sexual harassment in an office hallway. A key feature of experimental work using VR is drastic improvements in external and ecological validity – VR allows researchers to transition experiments from measuring how participants self-report they would react in the real-world to measuring how they actually behave when confronted with a scenario literally in front of their eyes. While alluring, the design, coding, and implementation of studies using VR adds technical complexity to projects and care must be taken to be intentional throughout the process. In this manuscript, we provide guidance to management scholars to understanding VR, its potential applications, and the considerations one must undertake when creating studies using VR. Overall, we advocate the use of VR by management researchers in their work and introduce both a roadmap and best practices to jump-start such endeavors.

Keywords: Virtual reality; laboratory methods; validities; technology; laboratory design; study design

Delving Deep
Research Methodology in Strategy and Management, Volume 15, 57–84
Copyright © 2025 Timothy D. Hubbard and Michael Villano
Published under exclusive licence by Emerald Publishing Limited
ISSN: 1479-8387/doi:10.1108/S1479-838720240000015004

INTRODUCTION

Laboratory methods are critical for strategy and management studies (Bitektine et al., 2020; Stevenson et al., 2020). Through experiments, we can test management theories with the goal of establishing causality. Indeed, some of the most important conclusions in the management field have come from laboratory studies which feature random assignment, manipulation of independent variables, and control over the experimental environment (Cook & Campbell, 1979; Kerlinger & Lee, 2000). Each of these factors leads to both high internal validity and statistical conclusion validity. However, as a community of scholars we should always be looking for new techniques to test theories in ways that enhance existing methods and overcome limitations.

As a methodological platform, virtual reality (VR) has the exciting potential to present new ways for management scholars to test theories (Pierce & Aguinis, 1997) and phenomena (Hubbard & Aguinis, 2023). VR is a "type of human-computer interface that allows users to become immersed in a computer-generated environment" (Hubbard & Aguinis, 2023, p. 1). VR users wear headsets with small computer screens close to their eyes and speakers close to their ears. The headsets are spatially tracked and the screens are updated based on the position and orientation of the head. Rather than taking a text-based Qualtrics survey or watching a video on a flat screen as one would observe the world through a window, participants can "step through the door" and be fully immersed in a virtual environment. Examples of virtual environments are innumerable: from corporate boardrooms to television sets and job interview rooms, almost any environment can be simulated. Unfortunately, VR is hard to describe to those who have not yet experienced it. Indeed, we liken describing virtual reality on paper to writing a vivid and accurate description of a color television to someone who has never seen a TV.

The purpose of this chapter is to advocate conducting laboratory studies using VR to management researchers. And, if interested in pursuing this path, we provide the reader with a base of knowledge to start. We make design, software, and hardware suggestions and discuss best practices from both the field and our own work. In terms of scope, however, we stop short of teaching how to code VR simulations. Instead, we encourage those interested in learning more to explore the large amount of training currently available. With each passing day, this technology becomes more accessible both technically and financially. If it feels daunting today, just return to your research idea in the near future.[1]

Given these goals, we make several key contributions to the field of strategy and management research. First, we provide a clear definition and conceptualization of VR for the field to enable researchers, developers, and reviewers to have a common scope for what constitutes a promising VR study. Second, we provide a clear discussion of the benefits and drawbacks of implementing studies in VR. These benefits and limitations are categorized into factors for both internal and external validity. Most external validity points consider ecological validity, or whether the study findings will generalize to real-life settings. Third, we provide a series of development practices that can help ground researchers, developers, and reviewers to a common set of criteria to accelerate the development and assessment of VR simulations. Finally, we provide a discussion of ethical concerns and recommendations for reviewers. In total, it is our hope that this manuscript can help speed the adoption of VR into management studies to help push the field forward in a meaningful way.

VIRTUAL REALITY (VR) DEFINED AND CONTEXTUALIZED FOR MANAGEMENT STUDIES

Researchers across disciplines such as psychology (Boydstun et al., 2021; Rizzo et al., 2021; Zimmer et al., 2019), medicine (Baghaei et al., 2021; Carroll et al., 2021; Eshuis et al., 2021), human–computer interaction (Dzardanova et al., 2022; Sterna et al., 2021), and education (Abich et al., 2021; Nesenbergs et al., 2020; Shorey & Ng, 2021) are already using VR in studies. VR is a computer tool wherein a person can be placed in an artificial environment through the simulation of sensory stimuli such as sight, sound, and touch. VR "creates an illusion that a person is in a different place" (Greengard, 2019) where they can participate in virtual experiences. VR experiences can be as realistic or imaginative as the researcher desires. One could as easily be placed in a corporate boardroom as a factory floor.

VR experiences can have different levels of physical interaction. For example, the headset may just rotate with the participant's head – 3 degrees of freedom. The position of the head doesn't move, but the user can look around at the environment. Alternatively, the headset could also track the position of the headset in three-dimensional (3D) space, allowing for the head to move throughout the virtual space – 6 degrees of freedom. Such room-scale (6 degrees of freedom), simulations are natural for participants to interact with and match real-world movements. While 3 degrees of freedom – such as simulations using 360° video – allow participants to look around, the location of their point of view is fixed in the environment. Room-scale simulations allow participants to stand up, walk around, and interact with objects in the virtual environment.

Before going into greater detail on the benefits, drawbacks, and applications of VR, we highlight a few salient points specifically for management researchers. While our community of scholars works to build and test a body of theory, the field of management is fundamentally linked to business practice – whether that is workers doing their jobs, entrepreneurs starting companies, CEOs leading companies, or stakeholders reacting to firm actions. Thus, when considering where VR can enhance laboratory studies, the options are seemingly limitless: nearly every interaction that workers, leaders, and stakeholders experience throughout their day are all opportunities to study. Table 1 provides ideas for the type of settings that can be simulated in VR. For example, strategy scholars could simulate board meetings, all-employee meetings, or media interviews. One could imagine that instead of having participants read hypothetical questions from a reporter and then type out responses, a researcher could simulate an entire television studio and have a virtual confederate play the part of a news anchor

Table 1. Summary of Potential Research Settings, Benefits of VR, and Data Collection.

Potential Management Research Settings	Core Benefits of VR	Data Collection Opportunities
Strategic Management:	*Validities:*	*Participant Behaviors:*
• All-employee meetings	• High external and ecological validity through realistic tasks and environments	• Decisions and survey items administered in headset
• Analyst meetings		• Object manipulation (handling a product)
• Board of directors meetings	• High internal validity through experimental control	• Avoidance (walking around objects)
• CEO media interviews in TV studios	*Activities:*	*Unobtrusive Behavioral Measures:*
• Floor of New York Stock Exchange	• Realistic work setting	• Decision speed
• Shareholder meetings	• Realistic work tasks	• Proximity to objects and virtual confederates
• Top management team meetings	• Can interact with objects – such as picking up a coffee cup	• Body movement
Organizational Behavior:	*Environmental Control:*	• Audio recordings and associated transcripts (content, tone, pace)
• Job interviews	• Immersive environments that are purpose-designed for a particular study	*Physiological Measurement:*
• Nonworks situations	• Realistic virtual environment	• Eye tracking (visual attention)
• Subordinate meetings	• Ability to manipulate environmental features (such as time of day)	• Electrodermal activity (arousal)
• Supervisor meetings	*Virtual Confederates:*	• Electroencephalogram (EEG)
• Team meetings	• Manipulate characteristics (gender, race)	• Facial expression (expressed emotions)
• Work tasks	• Manipulate behaviors (body language, lip sync, animation)	• Respiration
• Workplace encounters	• Perfectly consistent behaviors across participants	• Heart rate
Entrepreneurship:	*Audio Control:*	• Skin temperature
• Entrepreneurial pitches	• Consistency of speech characteristics between conditions (words, tenor, tone, pace)	
• Ideation sessions	• Consistent audio features (sound effects)	
• Investor meetings		
• Media interviews		

asking questions. This is one of the most straightforward benefits of using VR in studies: we can observe actual behavior, not behavioral intentions, in a highly controlled environment that better matches real-world business environments and activities.

Table 1 also provides a summary of the core benefits of VR for empirical work and potential data collection opportunities.

BENEFITS AND LIMITATIONS OF EMPLOYING VR IN MANAGEMENT STUDIES

The goals of using VR in management research are twofold: (1) to test theories that would otherwise be either challenging or untestable, and (2) to improve the validity of laboratory work. As Oxley et al. (2022, p. 1) note, "virtual reality is beneficial from a research and education perspective as it allows the assessment of participants in situations that would otherwise be ethically and practically difficult or impossible to study in the real world." We specifically believe management studies conducted using VR can benefit external, ecological, and internal validity.

VR: Improving External and Ecological Validity

External validity concerns "how strong a statement the experimenter can make about the generalizability of the results of the study" (Kerlinger & Lee, 2000, p. 479). Ecological validity assesses how generalizable findings are to the real world. VR has the ability for management and strategy scholars conducting laboratory work to overcome a common criticism: that laboratory studies are devoid of realism and, thus, have low external validity – regardless of empirical evidence to the contrary (e.g., Mitchell, 2012).

A Focus on Ecological Validity. VR can help improve ecological validity because it can simulate real business contexts, manipulate variables that one would experience in real life, and study business practices in a way that matches the real world. For example, instead of having participants read vignettes and rate the likelihood of their taking certain actions, they can experience a situation and choose how they behave in the moment (Aguinis & Bradley, 2014). This is the difference between reading a scenario about a company experiencing a crisis – an oil spill, product safety recall, or a workplace shooting – or experiencing the event – seeing the animals covered in oil, observing how customers could be hurt by a product, or standing in the lobby of the corporate offices surrounded by police cars and ambulances.

Psychological Realism. These crisis management examples can help scholars improve the ecological validity of their work by increasing the psychological realism of studies. Colquitt (2008, p. 618) notes that "a number of factors can promote psychological realism, including placing participants in real rather than hypothetical situations, using vivid and engrossing manipulations and tasks, and creating real stakes by using monetary or credit-based contingencies." There is a trade-off between mundane realism – how much an experiment is similar to everyday life situations – and experimental control. The more researchers can increase the realism and design experiments such that they mimic real life, the higher the psychological realism of their study. VR can completely reshape our existing relationship between balancing experimental control and the realism of the simulation (see Fig. 1).

Real-World Environments. Another way to achieve external validity is to put people in the most appropriate environment to test a particular theory. VR can help in this regard because participants can be placed in almost any imaginable environment including difficult-to-access as well as dangerous environments. VR can, for example, transport people to the floor of the New York Stock Exchange, the control room of a nuclear power plant, or the boardroom of a Fortune 100 company. This experience can be achieved without having to physically transport participants to the actual location. Participants can also be placed on stage in a

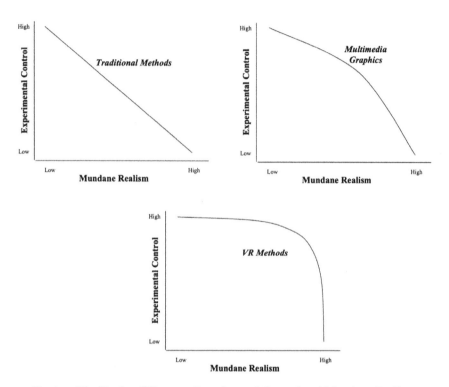

Fig. 1.   The Trade-off Between Experimental Control and Mundane Realism.
Source: Reproduced from Blascovich et al. (2002).

full lecture hall without needing real people in the room. Or, if a theory is best tested in a dangerous environment, researchers can place participants in that environment without subjecting them to physical risks.[2]

VR: Improving Internal Validity

For management scholars, VR has specific benefits to improve the internal validity of their studies – or "how strongly the experimenter can state the effect of the independent variable on the dependent variable" (Kerlinger & Lee, 2000, p. 478). Using VR, management scholars are forced to choose almost every aspect of the participant experience: they control the virtual environments, virtual confederates, sounds, animations, haptic feedback, and more. Everything a participant sees or hears – from the time of day out the window to the color of the walls – must be chosen. With each design element available for VR, management researchers, reviewers, and readers can be more confident that the relationship between the manipulation and the outcome is internally valid.

Using Virtual Confederates. Some traditional lab experiments use confederates – individuals brought in by experimenters to act as bystanders, participants, or teammates. In VR, we can use virtual confederates – avatars simulated in the software – as an alternative to humans. Real human confederates may not be needed. Instead of human confederates – who are unlikely to behave in the exact same way for every single participant (Kuhlen & Brennan, 2013) – we can program virtual confederates in VR. Because we choose exactly what they look like, what they say, and how they are animated, we know they will behave in the exact same way for each participant. If an organizational behavior scholar, for example, wanted to study supervisors dismissing employees, the employees in the study would have the exact same body language, tone of voice, and response from participant to participant. To provide a sense for how realistic virtual confederates can be, Fig. 2 provides photos of some we have used in VR.

Control Over the Environment. Consistent environments are important in experimentation. Studies implemented in VR can ensure that the environment is identical from participant to participant. This avoids confounds that may be present in real-world laboratories. If, for example, an experimenter uses a real-world laboratory with a window, participants will be exposed to different weather and lighting as the seasons and days progress. While such factors might be accounted for through random assignment, being able to control the environment can reduce noise in the study. In addition, a single lab room can function

Fig. 2. Examples of Virtual Confederates. *Note:* Created with Reallusion's Character Creator 4.

as many different physical spaces from boardrooms and offices to a warehouse with appropriate ambient sound that does not vary between participants (unless sound is part of the experimental manipulation). While in the past researchers have gone to great lengths to create realistic environments – such as building a casino (Blascovich et al., 1973) – VR can make varied, realistic environments much more accessible and cost-effective.

WHEN TO APPLY VR TO MANAGEMENT STUDIES

There are five broad features of studies that can especially benefit from employing VR. First, VR allows us to test theories that we either cannot or that would be difficult to test in the laboratory. Certain phenomena in the real world are difficult to recreate even in lab settings (Hubbard & Aguinis, 2023). For example, studying how people respond when they watch someone inappropriately touch or harass another person in the work environment, or when they are participating in discussions about controversial boardroom topics such as CEO dismissal, ethical lapses, or product recalls. In the case of sexual harassment, for example, a virtual confederate can inappropriately touch another virtual confederate – instead of relying on human confederates to model inappropriate behavior that could pose ethical challenges for the research team.

Second, VR allows us to test theories and phenomena that have not happened. Some researchers have done this without using VR by using laboratory experiments to understand future corporate governance changes (Krause et al., 2014). While pen-and-paper scenarios were appropriate for Krause et al. (2014), other upcoming phenomena might present challenges to such methods. Specifically, behavioral changes that are happening in the world can present opportunities that are ideal for VR-based methods. An example can be employees working with robots – a phenomenon that will become increasingly prevalent over time. While a researcher could study these future interactions using vignette designs – reading and reacting to a scenario about interacting with such robots – these methods have limitations (Aguinis & Bradley, 2014). In a VR world, a researcher could experimentally manipulate and vary the robots with which a participant interacts. These variations could include physical size, race, gender, attractiveness, and behavior of the robot without the need to purchase or program a single physical robot – all while presenting more realistic scenarios than pen-and-paper methods.

Third, VR allows us to safely observe the participants in dangerous scenarios. Participant safety is paramount in ethical laboratory research. VR can play an important role if testing a particular theory necessitates observing participants in situations where they feel a sense of danger or fear such as team management in search and rescue or emergency operations. VR is capable of delivering such high levels of immersion and presence that fear can be elicited (Diemer et al., 2015). For this reason, observing the management of police response in active shooter situations could be a good application for VR. VR systems can be set up as multiplayer simulations where participants can be in both the same physical and virtual environment (Christensen et al., 2018). Thus, multiple participants can participate in the same simulation.

Fourth, real-world situations that are expensive are good candidates for VR simulations. While there are upfront and ongoing expenses for VR systems, these costs can easily be balanced by the cheaper implementation of certain scenarios and their reuse in subsequent studies. Anything a management scholar can imagine can be built in VR. VR can transport participants anywhere in the world. As illustrated in Table 1, for example, a strategy scholar could simulate an all-employee meeting taking place at a corporate retreat. Conducting a study in a real physical conference center would likely be cost prohibitive. Or, when studying corporate boardroom interactions, a strategy researcher could build a physical boardroom at a significant cost or create a virtual environment of the same fidelity at a much lower expense.

Finally, VR allows participants to experience rare situations – abusive supervision, sexual harassment, workplace accidents, or active shooter situations, among others. When a situation is uncommon, researchers can spend a great deal of time waiting to observe it in the field. And, when such a rare situation does arise, it is unlikely to be randomly assigned. Endogeneity can enter field studies where something else likely induces the rare condition a researcher hopes to study. On the other hand, VR can help management scholars by randomly assigning the occurrence of such rare events.

Limitations of Using VR in Studies

While there are numerous benefits, it is necessary that management scholars take stock of several limitations to VR. The main hurdle in implementing VR in laboratory studies is the technical knowledge required to develop the software to conduct the studies. At this point, developing custom simulations requires deep knowledge of development in real-time 3D game engines such as those used to develop video games.[3] There are special considerations – discussed below – that researchers must consider when developing VR simulation software that go beyond what is typically needed in 3D simulation development, which is yet again more complicated than simple 2D or text-based scenarios.

There are also upfront cost considerations for hardware, software, and the physical space to conduct the studies. Researchers need access to headset hardware, which can vary in cost depending on needs, discussed below. Headsets can differ in their features such as visual fidelity, refresh rates, audio quality, eye tracking, and face tracking. Each desired feature will, of course, add costs. Researchers also might need specialized software to write the simulation, design digital environments, and create, rig, and animate virtual confederates. Further costs may be incurred if researchers want to collect biometric data such as electrodermal activity, heart rate, or respiratory data (Knaust et al., 2022). While some may view these costs as high, they must be considered in comparison to the costs of conducting studies without VR. As discussed above, it can be prohibitively costly to transport participants to specific locations or impractical to have them interact with expensive equipment.

DEVELOPMENT PRACTICES FOR VR

Developing a comprehensive, immersive VR experience may involve the creation of various digital elements such as the simulated environment, programming logic, human-like avatars, avatar animations, VR user interaction, audio (ambient or background sounds and speech), and haptic (touch) interactions. In this section, we provide management scholars a view into the different systems that makeup VR, along with best practices from other scholars and our own work in VR.

VR Development: Virtual Environments

Real-time 3D engines are available that allow for the integration of all elements of the VR experience into a distributable VR application (e.g., Unity and Unreal Engine). These platforms provide management scholars with all the functionality necessary to construct a virtual world. In addition to what is already in the engines, 3D objects and landscapes can be built using third-party modeling tools (e.g., 3D Studio Max, Maya, and Blender) or purchased from various 3D asset repositories. For example, a complete boardroom scene which includes a fully constructed boardroom along with a conference table, chairs, artwork, and lighting can be purchased from the Unity Asset Store. See Fig. 3 for some examples of premade virtual environments.

Even if a developer of a VR environment begins with a purchased asset, once it is in the engine it can be customized. For example, there are many websites dedicated to providing free or for-pay materials, such as wood grain images that could be used to customize the look of a corporate conference table. Walls, ceilings, and floors can be customized as well with the application of other materials and textures. Research has shown that people can recognize materials and textures accurately in VR (Niu & Lo, 2022). The lighting of VR environments can be adjusted through the application of lighting types commonly found in the real world – from spotlights and emissive lighting fixtures to adjusting the "sun" to simulate the time of day. The fidelity of VR environments can be improved through the addition of small details by importing 3D models of everyday items, such as lamps, books, potted plants, and coffee mugs, among others. One way to start designing a 3D environment is to take a photo of the real environment during the scenario of interest – for example, take a picture of a conference room during a meeting. You'll be able to see what is on the table and how messy the table really is – the virtual world should be just as messy as these reference images depict.

Environments that match real-world environments with high fidelity can increase the psychological realism and give researchers more confidence that their conclusions will generalize to the working world.

VR Development: User Interactions

Once a VR environment has been constructed, there may be several ways in which both the researcher and the participant under study would need to interact with it. Within the simulation, there are many ways in which a participant could interact with the environment. Participants can directly manipulate objects in the

INIRROR OFFICE ARCHVIZ by INIRROR on the Unity Asset Store

Office Interior Archviz by INIRROR on the Unity Asset Store

Modern Supermarket by AndragorInc on the UnityAsset Store

Church 2 by Dexssoft Games on the Unity Asset Store

Fig. 3. Examples of 3D Environments.

environment: open a door, pick up a book, or turn on a light. For research purposes, text can be present on screens in view of the participant to give instructions regarding the study or provide educational content, and a laser pointer can be employed to allow participants to press buttons to advance text as well as to manipulate sliders to respond to research questions on a Likert scale. Menu and interface design is an important consideration in VR studies (Wang et al., 2021). These participant interactions and responses can be recorded and written out in data files for later analysis. Having precise measurements and interactions can increase internal validity and reduce noise in the study. For example, instead of a survey completed at the end of an experiment, researchers in VR can administer questionnaires in the middle of situations – essentially pausing a scenario to obtain feedback.

VR Development: Audio

Audio can be utilized in a variety of ways to enhance the feeling of immersion in VR environments (Cooper et al., 2018). Virtual confederates can give speeches or directions in virtual meetings with either voice-actor or text-to-speech generated audio clips that can be lip synced to the confederate. Ambient sounds can be integrated to intensify the sense of being in a meeting room with subtle street noise and a slight ventilation hum.

Care should be taken when planning and implementing audio design in VR (Somberg, 2021). Like other portions of development, audio is a blank slate when you start a project. It is up to the researcher to select and implement each and every sound the participant will experience. A good way to get a feel for audio implementation in VR is to close one's eyes and make notes of all the sounds heard – traffic noise outside the window, people talking outside your office, and the hum of the ventilation system. One can imagine the difference between reading about angry investors in a vignette study compared to hearing angry people shouting questions at you at a shareholder meeting.

Somberg (2021) lays out three categories of sounds to consider. First, there are sounds from the world which include the environment (e.g., ambient sounds), weather (e.g., rain or wind), particle effects (e.g., fire or sparks), and physics (e.g., objects sliding against each other or collisions). Second, character sounds include the speech, movement, and interactions of all characters in the experience. Finally, the third is feedback sounds that include audio cues for feedback in menus and other sounds intended to enrich the user experience. Feedback sounds should help give confidence to the participant that they are interacting in the correct way.

Once the sound design has been planned, researchers must consider the technical choices of implementation and how those choices will influence the overall fidelity of the auditory system (Al-Jundi & Tanbour, 2022). Three factors can increase the fidelity of the auditory system in VR studies. First, is the quality of the auditory stimuli which correspond to the other cues a participant is experiencing. One such cue could include the participant's visual system: if they see a fire, they should hear a fire. It can also correspond to interactions a participant experiences: if a participant drops a cup, they should hear it hit the ground. Anytime the quality of the auditory stimuli suffers, researchers risk participants breaking immersion as their brain tries to understand why something did not happen or why it was different than they expected. The second factor is the realism of the surrounding audio. This realism reflects the degree to which the audio is an accurate reproduction of real-world sounds. The greater the correspondence between audio in the study and real-world audio, the greater the participant will accept the virtual reality as real. Finally, the third factor for audio fidelity is audio resolution, which refers to the degree of exactness with which the overall audio system reflects the real world. That is, rather than the accuracy of the individual sounds – whether a tin cup falling on the floor sounds like a tin cup – audio resolution focuses on the entire system. In real-time 3D systems, audio spatializers can be used to increase audio fidelity. These systems can control the position of the audio such that the sounds come from particular locations. There can also be room effects such as reverb (the audio bounces off surfaces in a realistic way), occlusion (objects can block sound), and decay (audio falls off as the distance between the participant and the source increase).

Such subtleties in audio design help increase immersion and presence (Al-Jundi & Tanbour, 2022). The key part of audio design, much like the other design considerations, is control. Every sound must be selected and implemented individually. And, thus, every participant will be exposed to the sounds chosen by the researcher. Detailed consideration put into strong audio design and implementation can help improve the participant experience and help melt the divide between the virtual world and the real world.

VR Development: Haptic Feedback

Haptics are physical feedback through touch sensations (Al-Jundi & Tanbour, 2022). Enabling the sense of touch in an immersive VR environment involves a broad spectrum of touch experiences from the simplicity of vibrating the VR game controller to providing realistic feelings of real-world texture through a haptic glove. Full-body haptic suits can provide physical sensation from the shoulders down to the ankles. Haptics can provide important biofeedback for participants. It can help them know that they can pick something up. It can also help confirm that participants are interacting with objects or menus. A slight vibration when a button is pushed can help the user know what to do. Haptics can also help simulate the pressure participants feel when they touch objects in VR. Through purposeful haptic design, participants can feel the rumble of machinery in a factory, the touch of a virtual confederate, or the menu with which they are interacting.

VR Development: Virtual Confederates

Virtual confederates, human or otherwise, can be present in the environment and programmed to move in realistic ways (Fysh et al., 2022). These realistic movements can include body movements as well as lip sync to match their speech. These confederates can be created with third-party software tools that allow for high levels of fidelity as well as customization. Fig. 2 provides some examples of current virtual confederates used in VR. While at times the researchers should create their own avatars, online stores enable researchers to purchase human avatars of different body types, genders, and races. All aspects of the virtual confederates' appearance can be manipulated, from eye color and hairstyle to body shape and all aspects of clothing and accessories, which are also available for purchase at modest cost and customizable by modifying colors, textures, and virtual fabrics. These digital assets afford great creativity; for example, an organizational behavior scholars interested in studying discrimination based on body type could experimentally manipulate the body mass of a virtual confederate and observe participant behaviors directed towards those individuals.

VR Development: Locomotion

The choice of locomotion methods can impact the degree to which participants experience simulator or cyber sickness. The traditional recommendation for VR environments that can be "walked" include physically walking over short distances (less than a few meters) in a room-scale environment, using teleportation, or employing omnidirectional treadmills. Such treadmills enable participants to move in 360°, which can also help improve simulator experience by providing a more direct mapping between physical movement and the movement experienced in the VR environment.

The choice of locomotion method depends on the requirements of the study while balancing issues such as simulator sickness. The three primary methods of loco-motion – (1) walking within the virtual space, (2) continuous locomotion such as free stick-based movements, and (3) discrete locomotion such as teleportation – all have different trade-offs. Real-world movements such as walking around are the most natural for participants (Christensen et al., 2018) and should be the goal for VR developers. If the participant can locomote on their own – either through a small virtual world or a large play area – that is the most natural and will lead to the lowest simulator sickness, highest immersion, and highest presence. However, these small-scale environments are not always feasible. If control-based locomotion is needed because the physical VR space is too small or the virtual world is too big, continuous locomotion is an option. In this case, participants use a joystick on their controller to move (virtually while standing still) or a 360 treadmill that provides a step-to-step correspondence to walking or running. The benefit to continuous movement is that there is no break in immersion, but studies have found this to have relatively higher levels of simulator sickness (Frommel et al., 2017). Finally, teleport locomotion "elicited least discomfort and provided the highest scores for enjoyment, presence, and affective state" (Frommel et al., 2017, p. 1). Some studies, such as participating in a board room meeting while seated at a conference room table, require no locomotion at all.

VR Development: Reducing Simulator Sickness

Simulator sickness – or VR sickness when specifically considered for VR – is "bodily discomfort associated with a series of symptoms such as disorientation, nausea, vomiting, and visual fatigue" (Chen & Weng, 2022, p. 817). Simulator sickness is a health and safety risk for VR studies. Simulator sickness occurs when your brain thinks you are moving, but your body is static. This disconnect causes enough confusion to make someone feel ill. Simulator sickness, however, does not have one clear cause. Chen and Weng (2022) catalog that the duration in VR, time lags, a poor field of view, display content, gender, and age may contribute to simulator sickness.

Good tracking is critically important in VR to reduce the likelihood and severity of simulator sickness (Caserman et al., 2021). With good tracking, the likelihood of simulator sickness is greatly decreased. Fortunately, this is an area of rapid advancement for headset manufacturers and should continue to improve over time. Poor tracking usually manifests as either the headset position doesn't match the participant's real head position or the controllers and hands don't match their physical location. Both of these situations quickly induce simulator sickness. One can imagine the discomfort of seeing their virtual hand float off into space while their real hand is stationary, or a room turns sideways while their head is still.

Researchers and developers can work to reduce simulator sickness by having a wide field of view when a participant is stationary but restricting that field of view when moving (Teixeira & Palmisano, 2021). They can also ensure that the only head movement is based on the participants' actual motions. When a participant needs to move fast – like flying through the air or going up – they should be placed within a stable reference such as a plane or elevator.

Researchers and developers should test their simulation software on the target hardware – the headsets and computers that will actually run the simulation – throughout development. By continually testing, it will become apparent when these issues arise. Normal development cycles include building up the simulation from simple models to the full simulation. Developers can more easily diagnose issues if they notice video or tracking issues throughout development as the VR simulation becomes more and more complex. When the software begins to slow down frame rates or drop frames, developers can use profiling software to locate the bottleneck. Typically, this is either the central processing unit (CPU) or graphics processing unit (GPU). Profiling software will show how each frame is processed including what must run on both the CPU and GPU. Resolving these issues is beyond the scope of this guide but knowing that profiling exists can help researchers optimize their simulations.

VR Development: Accessibility

VR poses an exciting opportunity for management researchers to design experiments that increase the accessibility of studies to people with accessibility challenges.

VR can help participants with mobility challenges by allowing them to pick up objects at a distance, a design concept called remote grab. When designed, implemented, and enabled, remote grab allows participants to use a raycast – a laser beam from the controller or their hand – to select an object from a distance and pull it to themselves. Thus, rather than needing to walk across a room to pick up an object, participants can grab it from where they are at the moment. For participants with mobility challenges, this represents an opportunity to design the study so that they are able to participate.

Unlike the real world, researchers and programmers can also design VR interactions such that only one hand is needed potentially increasing the pool of potential participants. Sometimes objects require two hands because of the dimensions or weight. With one-handed interactions, the dimensions of an object are somewhat irrelevant. The object can be snapped or locked to a hand in any position. The weight of an object also becomes irrelevant – in VR, if a researcher wishes, participants can pick up a sledgehammer with one hand and wield it as though it were a pencil.[4]

Finally, researchers can consider using closed captioning within the virtual environment. Many times, researchers choose to exclude potential participants who have hearing impairments. This might be necessary at times given some study designs require verbal prompts or verbal responses, but in general, VR may help overcome this accessibility limitation using closed captioning. Closed captioning can be used to show the text that virtual confederates are using to allow the participant to follow along without hearing the audio. Closed captioning can also be placed around objects. For example, there could be a prompt above a laser pointer that says "Pick me up" to prompt the user to grab the pointer.

VR Development: Olfactory System

Technologies to present VR environment appropriate smells are available with limited subsets of smells designed for a particular simulated situation (Serrano et al., 2016). For example, in a health and wellness meditation study, the olfactory system could deploy calming smells (forest, beach, etc.) to the participant to enhance mood. Military and first responder simulations could prepare participants for warfare and emergency situations by presenting smells of the battlefield or a fire (Lefrak, 2022). While this area of technology and research is still nascent, it is becoming more advanced and accessible.

VR Development: Important Survey Scales

There are several survey scales that can be considered in VR studies to understand the participant and simulation experience.

Simulator Sickness. First, as discussed above, simulator sickness is a phenomenon of which researchers need to be aware. Measures of simulator sickness came out of the military who needed to evaluate aviators' training protocols. The Simulator Sickness Questionnaire (SSQ) was developed in the early 1990s (Kennedy et al., 1993) and later reexamined (Balk et al., 2013). Simulator sickness has three distinct symptoms: oculomotor (e.g., eyestrain, difficulty focusing, blurred vision, headache); disorientation (e.g., dizziness, vertigo), and nausea (e.g., nausea, stomach awareness, increased salivation, burping). The SSQ's list of individual symptoms is aggregated to provide the three overall symptoms.

Presence. Igroup Presence Questionnaire (IPQ) (Schubert et al., 2001, p. 266) measures the "sense of being in the virtual environment" and is operationalized by subscales measuring general presence, spatial presence, involvement, and realness (Kisker et al., 2021). This scale can help researchers contextualize how well their simulation engrosses the participant by allowing them to feel present in the virtual environment.

Game Experience. The Game Experience Questionnaire (IJsselsteijn et al., 2013) can help measure competence, immersion, flow, tension, challenge, negative affect, and positive affect in the VR. While this scale has been criticized (Law et al., 2018), it is still widely used.

Technology Anxiety. Technology anxiety is concerned with "the level of stress and anxiety about technological devices in general and about making mistakes when using them" (Knaust et al., 2022, p. 930). Technology anxiety can be measured using a four item subscale of the Technology Usage Inventory (Kothgassner et al., 2013).

It is not necessary to measure all these scales in every VR study. Instead, they can help provide context to studies and identify issues. For example, if researchers measure the SSQ in a study, they can monitor the measurement early in the study. If SSQ is higher than mean levels reported in other studies or if there is something unusual going on, the researchers can try to identify the root cause and address it.

VR Development: Unobtrusive Measurements

Beyond the survey scales just discussed, there are many other measurements that can be considered in VR studies. Researchers benefit from VR "on several fronts as data collection is covert, continuous, passive, and occurs within a controlled context" (Yaremych & Persky, 2019, p. 1). Two important features of unobtrusive measurement are that they are covert and continuous. Researchers and programmers must consider what unobtrusive measures they will need ahead of time, as they will typically have to develop the software in a way to record and save the data. By default, real-time 3D engines do not save any data – everything must be considered and integrated ahead of time. Table 1 provides examples of the types of measurements management scholars can choose to implement.

Measuring Eye Gaze. Tracking a participant's gaze is of vital interest to researchers (Meißner & Oll, 2019). Screen-based eye tracking is a standard and acceptable method of understanding a participant's gaze. While we can gain important insights from visual attention on a 2D plane, researchers are more and more interested in understanding visual attention in the broader world. Researchers are currently using eye tracking glasses. Analyzing the data from these devices is difficult as the researcher must match the eye gaze data with the video recorded from the front of the glasses. Eye tracking is more straightforward to handle in VR. There are two methods for eye tracking based on either headset direction or an eye tracker integrated into the headset. Using the direction of the headset assumes that the participant's gaze is straight ahead. While there is obvious error in this measurement, the simplicity of it is appealing. In either method, researchers can use a ray trace out from the head position in the direction of the eye to determine what the participant is gazing at in any particular moment. These ray casts can then be aggregated based on game objects within the software. Thus, if visual attention of a particular virtual confederate in the virtual world is of interest to researchers, they can add up the time that the ray cast hits that object during the simulation. Dedicated eye tracking hardware coupled with a VR headset is likely more precise than other head mounted solutions such as matching up video with tracking data from eye tracking glasses. Eye tracking data can give management scholars a continuous view into participant visual attention.

Measuring Movement and Position. VR headsets and controllers are continually tracked. This tracking can be augmented by trackers placed on other parts of the body such as the participants' feet. Researchers can take advantage of position tracking by recording the movement of the headset, controllers, and hands. The movement and position data can be a valuable resource for researchers. Researchers can also record when body parts are in specific volumes in the virtual world. For example, a researcher could record if a user raises their hand in a meeting or if a participant reaches for an object. These unobtrusive measures have the potential to be quite revealing of human behavior.

Measuring Facial Expressions. Facial expressions have become an important part of management and strategy research (Hellmann et al., 2020). Facial expressions occur based on whether people feel a particular way, choose to express a particular emotion (even if they do not feel it), or do not express any emotion, regardless of how they may actually be feeling. Measurement of facial expressions in VR is becoming increasingly easier as technology improves. Many headset manufacturers are including facial expression cameras in their headsets to allow for avatars in social apps to accurately display their consumers' faces. Thus, when a consumer smiles in real life, their virtual avatar also smiles. This technology benefits researchers who can use the same facial expression camera to record these data throughout the study. One nuance to consider, though, is that most face trackers are used for the area around the mouth, while the eyebrows and forehead are obscured by the headset. Rather than relying on affect scales, facial expressions can provide insight into what emotions participants physically express. For example, one could determine if participants laugh at a CEO's jokes (e.g., Miron-Spektor et al., 2022).

VR DESIGN LESSONS LEARNED

We now go over some unscientific lessons that we have learned while developing and running studies in VR. While there might be ongoing research on these topics, published studies corroborating our experiences are lacking. Thus, presenting these lessons serves two purposes: one is to disseminate these lessons to aid developers and the other is to propose interesting VR-specific methods research topics. We have found that focusing on making many small improvements can drastically increase immersion and presence in VR while also reducing simulator sickness. It is hard to nail down exactly which change leads to the largest improvement.

First, when designing your environment keep in mind that very little in the real world is perfectly clean, straight, and neat. Instead, there is likely some dirt on the windows, scratches on the tables, and messy papers on the table.

Second, when designing the participant flow for the study, take some time to consider the start of the VR experience. Providing acclimation time – where participants can get used to wearing the headset and their surroundings – can help participants increase immersion. We have also found it helpful to have participants learn all the mechanics they will need to use in the simulation prior to participating in the experimental simulation. Participants who will use a laser pointer to make menu selections should have time to practice and ask questions of the researchers if they are confused. If participants need to pick up objects, have a few simple 3D cubes around to try. If they need to locomote, make sure they have a practice room in which to move around. It is beneficial to have the simulation only proceed when participants have demonstrated proficiency with the game mechanics. Immersion can be broken if they need to ask a question in the middle of a simulation.

Third, watching videos in VR simulations can increase immersion. Watching a short video on a TV or computer screen is such a natural act in the real world. If you can have instructional videos or filler videos in the VR environment, these can help the participant feel grounded in the VR world.

Fourth, if virtual confederates are speaking to a participant or listening to a participant, have them look the participant in the eye. Enabling this feature poses a technical challenge that will require some programming. This challenge can be overcome since the headset position of the participant is tracked and the eyes of the virtual confederates can be animated. There is something unnatural about someone not looking a person in the eye when they are speaking or listening.

Next, when coding the simulation, ensure that the simulation is coded in a way that keeps the frame rate somewhat higher than the desired frame rate on the target platform. Thus, if the target is 90fps, try to plan for 100fps. This overhead can help ensure that if something unexpected runs in the background, the simulation will maintain a high enough frame rate and lower the likelihood of simulator sickness.

We also recommend researchers save the data to both the cloud and a local hard drive. This is good practice for data backup. Saving data to the cloud enables researchers to check on the data collection from anywhere in the world. Many labs run on multiple computers and headsets. Cloud saves can be a central repository for the different computers and headsets running the simulation at the same time.

Finally, positional audio is important. We discussed audio in the development section above, but we wanted to revisit it. Whether the noise is related to venting, traffic, or people speaking, the position of the audio can help immensely. Positional audio is especially important if there are multiple virtual confederates and they are speaking. The human brain can much easier discern who is speaking when hearing the voice as it does in the real world. For example, when a speaker is at an angle to a participant, there is a slight delay and lower volume between the closer ear and the farther ear based on the distance between them on the head. Subtle differences such as audio decay are important for the brain and can help orient the participant to the correct speaker.

STEPS TO ADOPT VR INTO RESEARCH STREAMS: HEADSETS AND LABS

In this section, we provide a general process to integrate VR into research. These recommendations are based on running VR simulations built in real-time 3D engines as opposed to other options such as 360° video. Fig. 4 provides an overview and visual for how the different hardware and software come together to realize high-quality, immersive VR simulations. Table 2 provides pricing and

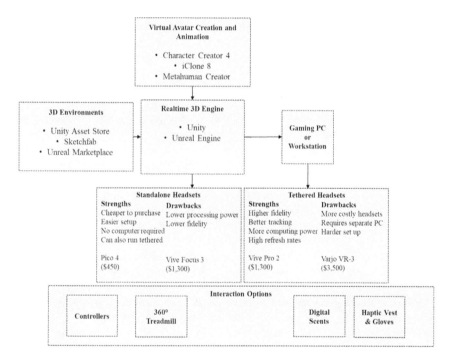

Fig. 4. Examples of Virtual Reality Technology Options. *Note:* The arrows indicate the flow of information and assets. For example, virtual confederates are created independently and then used within real-time 3D engines. And gaming PCs or workstations run the software for tethered headsets, while stand-alone headsets do not require a PC. The prices in this figure are as of January of 2023 and we readily acknowledge they are likely to change given this evolving industry.

Table 2. Sample Range of VR Configurations for Headset Hardware.

Headset	Computer Requirements	2023 Pricing
OpenBCI Galea ($22,500–$31,500) Varjo XR-3 or Aero headset with attached biometric sensors • Includes integrated biometric sensors (EEG, EOG, EMG, PPG, EDA, and eye tracking) • Extremely high fidelity with excellent tracking and high refresh rates • Includes automatic IPD adjustment • Requires purchase of base stations and controllers	i9 processor with Nvidia 4090 or better graphics card and 64 GB RAM (Alienware $5,000)	$27,500–$36,500 per seat
Varjo VR-3 Headset ($4,500) • Extremely high fidelity with excellent tracking and high refresh rates • Includes eye tracking and automatic IPD adjustment • Requires purchase of base stations and controllers • Requires software subscription	i9 processor with Nvidia 3090 or better graphics card and 64 GB RAM (Alienware $3,500)	$8,000 per seat
HTC Vive Pro 2 ($1,400) • Very high fidelity with excellent tracking and high refresh rates	Same as above	$5,000–$6,000 per seat
HTC Vive Focus 3 ($1,300) • Lower processing and graphics power when run stand-alone without a PC • Enterprise-grade, swappable batteries • Eye tracker and face tracker options	Stand-alone or tethered to gaming PC	$1,300 per seat
Pico 4 Enterprise ($1,000) • Lower processing and graphics power when run stand-alone without a PC • Enterprise-grade • Eye tracker and face tracker	Stand-alone or tethered to gaming PC	$1,000 per seat
Pico 4 ($500) • Lower processing and graphics power when run stand-alone without a PC • Consumer-grade	Stand-alone or tethered to gaming PC	$500 per seat

Note: IPD is interpupillary distance, the distance between the eyes.

discussion of current VR technology ranging from the highest end headsets with integrated biometric sensors to consumer-grade headsets that can run without a dedicated computer. Finally, Table 3 provides a menu of sorts with different software that researchers can use as they design their studies, including different real-time 3D game engines, locations to get virtual assets, sounds, and avatars.

In general, there are four steps to implement VR in studies. Some of these steps typically happen in parallel.

(1) *Identify a Developer:* The developer of the VR simulation can be the researcher or a game development professional or team. If researchers want to do it themselves, there are many resources that allow them to be

Table 3. Sample Software Tools for VR Implementation.

Software Tool	Purpose	Price
Unity	Real-time 3D engine	Free for research use
Unreal Engine	Real-time 3D engine	Free for research use
Unity Asset Store	Online store to acquire 3D assets	Some free assets, with many assets such as environments under $25
Unreal Marketplace	Online store to acquire 3D assets	Some free assets, with many assets such as environments under $25
Blender	3D modeling and object creation	Free
Character Creator & iClone	Human avatar editor and animator (also supports auto-lip sync)	$800 with educational discount
Adobe Mixamo	3D characters and animations	Free
GIMP	2D image manipulation for textures, such as wall styles (brick, stone, plaster, etc.)	Free
Audacity	Audio editor	Free
Replica Studios	AI-generated voice acting for Text-to-Speech	$25 for 4 hours
Freesound.org	Sound samples	Free
weloveindie	Sound samples	Free for educational uses

self-taught through online courses or video tutorials. Developers should be familiar with real-time 3D engines and developing software specifically for VR applications.

(2) *Design the Experiment:* This chapter can guide researchers through some of the fundamental choices they will have to make as they develop the design of the experiment. Using each section as a guidepost for what needs to be considered can help researchers document what they will need to develop.

(3) *Implementing the Experiment:* The VR simulation needs to be developed, prototyped, and tested at regular intervals to ensure that it is meeting the goals laid out in the experimental protocol. The more often the team works together to test the current state of a simulation, the greater the likelihood of success. Regular testing in headsets will ensure that the hard work being done will meet the expectations of the whole team.

(4) *Setting up a VR Laboratory:* While running VR studies through online services like Prolific are becoming more accessible, many researchers will opt to conduct the studies in their own laboratories. VR labs need to be set up with the appropriate VR hardware and software to run the completed experience. Room-scale VR needs at least a 3 m × 3 m room. Standing/seated VR requires a few feet in front of a desk. Tables 2 and 3 provide specific hardware and software recommendations as of this writing.

While this all may seem daunting, it should be viewed as a journey – the environments and simulations you develop to run in new laboratories can serve as a foundation for an almost limitless number of studies.

ETHICAL CONCERNS FOR VR STUDIES

There are several ethical concerns researchers need to consider as they design and implement studies using VR. Remember, according to Marvel Comics, "with great power there must also come – great responsibility."

The first ethical concern stems from the excitement of possibilities. So much can be done in VR that it might be enticing for researchers to put users in inappropriate situations. Specifically, because participants cannot be physically harmed in VR, researchers could put participants in situations where they could reasonably expect to be hurt in the real world. Examples of this could include having participants observing physical fights between customers and employees or having an active shooter in an office building. Such dangerous situations are all possible in VR, but this should not be an invitation to use such simulations without a clear purpose that exceeds the risk to the participant. Participants can still fall, trip over themselves, or suffer other adverse psychological effects.

Putting participants in apparent physical danger or extremely stressful situations might also trigger unintended psychological responses – such as triggering prior traumatic events or leading to post-traumatic stress disorder (PTSD). For example, Neyret et al. (2020) had participants complete the Milgram Obedience experiment. Caution must be taken. Institutional human subject review boards should be aware of these possibilities and serve as guardians, but researchers must design studies appropriately and not put the burden of responsibility on an outside regulatory group.

Another area of care that must be taken is the aforementioned simulator sickness. It is imperative that researchers develop their simulation software to minimize simulator sickness. Above we discussed ways to minimize simulator sickness and fortunately have had very few cases in our own lab having run hundreds of participants. Many participants are not aware of simulator sickness as a potential adverse condition – even if it is detailed in the consent form. Thus, the onus is on researchers to ensure that they have done enough work to reduce the likelihood of participants encountering issues. It is not possible to completely remove the possibility that someone will experience simulator sickness. The only exception to this is for researchers who are investigating simulator sickness either as an independent or dependent variable. In such cases, it is important for participants to have a clear understanding of the experience which they are agreeing to undergo.

RECOMMENDATIONS FOR REVIEWERS OF VR STUDIES

At this time, many management reviewers find it challenging to properly evaluate VR studies. Specifically, reviewers may not have been exposed to VR, and so it is hard for them to conceptualize the realism and immersion of the technology.

Reviewers, thus, may start from a position of aversion to VR technology. But even without having been in an immersive VR environment, there are some simple recommendations that can help reviewers effectively evaluate research using VR. The main consideration for reviewers is to increase the transparency of data and methods reported in VR studies (Lanier et al., 2019). Increasing the amount and quality of data and information about such studies is key, as it can provide the reviewer team with enough material to understand the totality of the VR simulations. A checklist for reviewers is provided in Table 4.

While one can imagine providing a printout of a Qualtrics survey experiment, it is much harder to show the merits of VR software to reviewers. It is challenging to easily provide reviewers with the experimental materials. Many reviewers do not have access to VR equipment and, when they do, VR software is often developed for the specific hardware being used in their specific laboratory. Thus, the VR simulation software might not run on a reviewer's specific headset. While this is a current limitation, many platforms are moving to consistent development environments (e.g., OpenXR), which should make it easier to run the same software on different devices. A reviewer not being able to run the software in a headset, though, is not a reasonable reason to negatively evaluate a particular study. Instead, the authors should provide screenshots and videos of the simulation. Reviewers who rely on screenshots and video though, will view them in the context of their 2D screen, which is much less immersive than being in a VR headset.

Researchers should also provide other materials used in the study including any surveys or debrief scripts used with participants. These materials can help contextualize the whole study and the experience of participants going through it. A timeline of events for participants is especially helpful so reviewers know when specific surveys were given and the order of events within the simulation. Finally, all the data and analysis files should be provided to help with transparency. The data and analysis files are also an opportunity for reviewers to answer their own questions. For example, if an author did not report a particular correlation a reviewer believes is important, the reviewer can use the data provided to run that particular correlation themselves. Including data and analysis files should speed

Table 4. A Checklist for Reviewers of VR Studies.

	Consideration	Evaluation
Software Availability	Was a copy of the VR software provided for the review team?	Yes/No
	Did the researchers specify what software and hardware is needed to run the software?	Yes/No
	Were screenshots and videos of the simulation provided for reviewers who are unable to run the software?	Yes/No
Data Transparency	Did the researcher provide the other materials for the study (e.g., surveys and debrief scripts)?	Yes/No
	Were the data files provided (such as de-identified Stata files)?	Yes/No
	Were the analyses files provided (e.g., Stata .do files)?	Yes/No

up the review process. Public data can also allow future readers the opportunity to scrutinize the data and analyses. The data can additionally help spur future research as scholars look at other, unexamined relationships that occur in the dataset.

CONCLUSION

The field of strategy and management is at an inflection point regarding the potential adoption of VR as a legitimate method of laboratory study. On the one path, we can remain skeptical and enact barriers to prevent VR studies from publication – through the review process, doctoral training, and public skepticism. On the other path, we can be open-minded about the strengths and limitations of VR in management research. The natural reaction that VR is unrealistic, not immersive, and does not lead to participant presence in the virtual world is already outdated. The hardware and software capabilities used in VR are ultrarealistic and are now only limited by the technical capabilities of the researcher and the programmers creating the simulations. Over time, these barriers will fall as well. If researchers come together now and accept VR as a legitimate methodology, we can drastically increase the types of theories we can test and increase both the internal and external validity of our conclusions.

NOTES

1. Compared with a few months ago, technologies such as ChatGPT are enabling developers to write code faster by providing a base code for a function of a simulation that can then be edited, refined, and optimized. While these technologies are not going to write a full simulation, they can be a great resource for learning and writing code faster.

2. Psychological risks should still be considered, see the Ethical Considerations section in the Discussion.

3. There are alternative approaches to VR simulations created using real-time 3D engines such as 360° video, which allow for easier entry, high immersion, and lower hardware requirements. Furthermore, there is off-the-shelf software that may be used such as VR conferencing solutions. The choice to use these products primarily centers around the level of presence and control a researcher requires. If a participant needs to be able to pick objects up or move around a room, real-time 3D engines are the most appropriate solutions.

4. Weight can also be designed into the simulation such that the physics behave in a way that requires participants to put effort into picking up and moving objects.

REFERENCES

Abich, J., Parker, J., Murphy, J. S., & Eudy, M. (2021). A review of the evidence for training effectiveness with virtual reality technology. *Virtual Reality*, *25*(4), 919–933.

Aguinis, H., & Bradley, K. J. (2014). Best-practice recommendations for designing and implementing experimental vignette methodology studies. *Organizational Research Methods*, *17*(4), 351–371.

Al-Jundi, H. A., & Tanbour, E. Y. (2022). A framework for fidelity evaluation of immersive virtual reality systems. *Virtual Reality*, *26*(3), 1103–1122.

Baghaei, N., Chitale, V., Hlasnik, A., Stemmet, L., Liang, H. N., & Porter, R. (2021). Virtual reality for supporting the treatment of depression and anxiety: Scoping review. *JMIR Mental Health*, *8*(9), e29681.

Balk, S., Bertola, M., & Inman, V. (2013, June). *Simulator sickness questionnaire: Twenty years later.* In *Driving Assessment Conference* (Vol. 7, No. 2013). University of Iowa.

Bitektine, A., Hill, K., Song, F., & Vandenberghe, C. (2020). Organizational legitimacy, reputation, and status: Insights from micro-level measurement. *Academy of Management Discoveries*, *6*(1), 107–136.

Blascovich, J., Loomis, J., Beall, A. C., Swinth, K. R., Hoyt, C. L., & Bailenson, J. N. (2002). Immersive virtual environment technology as a methodological tool for social psychology. *Psychological Inquiry*, *13*(2), 103–124.

Blascovich, J., Veach, T. L., & Ginsburg, G. P. (1973). Blackjack and the risky shift. *Sociometry*, *36*(1), 42.

Boydstun, C. D., Pandita, S., Finkelstein-Fox, L., & Difede, J. (2021). Harnessing virtual reality for disaster mental health: A systematic review. *Translational Issues in Psychological Science*, *7*(3), 315–331.

Carroll, J., Hopper, L., Farrelly, A. M., Lombard-Vance, R., Bamidis, P. D., & Konstantinidis, E. I. (2021). A scoping review of augmented/virtual reality health and wellbeing interventions for older adults: Redefining immersive virtual reality. *Frontiers in Virtual Reality*, *2*, 655338.

Caserman, P., Garcia-Agundez, A., Gámez Zerban, A., & Göbel, S. (2021). Cybersickness in current-generation virtual reality head-mounted displays: Systematic review and outlook. *Virtual Reality*, *25*(4), 1153–1170.

Chen, S., & Weng, D. (2022). The temporal pattern of VR sickness during 7.5-h virtual immersion. *Virtual Reality*, *26*(3), 817–822.

Christensen, J. V., Mathiesen, M., Poulsen, J. H., Ustrup, E. E., & Kraus, M. (2018). Player experience in a VR and non-VR multiplayer game. *Proceedings of the virtual reality international conference – Laval Virtual* (pp. 1–4).

Colquitt, J. A. (2008). From the editors publishing laboratory research in AMJ: A question of when, not if. *Academy of Management Journal*, *51*(4), 616–620.

Cook, T. D., & Campbell, D. T. (1979). *Quasi-experimentation: Design & analysis issues for field settings*. Houghton Mifflin.

Cooper, N., Milella, F., Pinto, C., Cant, I., White, M., & Meyer, G. (2018). The effects of substitute multisensory feedback on task performance and the sense of presence in a virtual reality environment. *PLoS One*, *13*(2), e0191846.

Diemer, J., Alpers, G. W., Peperkorn, H. M., Shiban, Y., & Mühlberger, A. (2015). The impact of perception and presence on emotional reactions: A review of research in virtual reality. *Frontiers in Psychology*, *6*.

Dzardanova, E., Kasapakis, V., Gavalas, D., & Sylaiou, S. (2022). Virtual reality as a communication medium: A comparative study of forced compliance in virtual reality versus physical world. *Virtual Reality*, *26*, 737–757. https://doi.org/10.1007/s10055-021-00564-9

Eshuis, L. V., van Gelderen, M. J., van Zuiden, M., Nijdam, M. J., Vermetten, E., Olff, M., & Bakker, A. (2021). Efficacy of immersive PTSD treatments: A systematic review of virtual and augmented reality exposure therapy and a meta-analysis of virtual reality exposure therapy. *Journal of Psychiatric Research*, *143*, 516–527.

Frommel, J., Sonntag, S., & Weber, M. (2017). Effects of controller-based locomotion on player experience in a virtual reality exploration game. *Proceedings of the 12th international conference on the foundations of digital games* (pp. 1–6).

Fysh, M. C., Trifonova, I. V., Allen, J., McCall, C., Burton, A. M., & Bindemann, M. (2022). Avatars with faces of real people: A construction method for scientific experiments in virtual reality. *Behavior Research Methods*, *54*, 1461–1475. https://doi.org/10.3758/s13428-021-01676-5

Greengard, S. (2019). *Virtual reality*. The MIT Press.

Hellmann, A., Ang, L., & Sood, S. (2020). Towards a conceptual framework for analysing impression management during face-to-face communication. *Journal of Behavioral and Experimental Finance*, *25*, 100265.

Hubbard, T. D., & Aguinis, H. (2023). Conducting phenomenon-driven research using virtual reality and the metaverse. *Academy of Management Discoveries*, *9*(3), 408–415. https://doi.org/10.5465/amd.2023.0031

IJsselsteijn, W. A., de Kort, Y. A. W., & Poels, K. (2013). *The game experience questionnaire.* Technische Universiteit Eindhoven.

Kennedy, R. S., Lane, N. E., Berbaum, K. S., & Lilienthal, M. G. (1993). Simulator sickness questionnaire: An enhanced method for quantifying simulator sickness. *The International Journal of Aviation Psychology*, *3*(3), 203–220.

Kerlinger, F. N., & Lee, H. B. (2000). *Foundations of behavioral research* (4th ed.). Harcourt College Publishers.

Kisker, J., Gruber, T., & Schöne, B. (2021). Behavioral realism and lifelike psychophysiological responses in virtual reality by the example of a height exposure. *Psychological Research*, *85*(1), 68–81.

Knaust, T., Felnhofer, A., Kothgassner, O. D., Höllmer, H., Gorzka, R. J., & Schulz, H. (2022). Exposure to virtual nature: The impact of different immersion levels on skin conductance level, heart rate, and perceived relaxation. *Virtual Reality*, *26*(3), 925–938.

Kothgassner, O. D., Felnhofer, A., Hauk, N., Kasthofer, E., Gomm, J., & KryspinExner, I. (2013). *TUI: Technology usage inventory.* FFG.

Krause, R., Whitler, K. A., & Semadeni, M. (2014). Power to the principals! An experimental look at shareholder say-on-pay voting. *Academy of Management Journal*, *57*(1), 94–115.

Kuhlen, A. K., & Brennan, S. E. (2013). Language in dialogue: When confederates might be hazardous to your data. *Psychonomic Bulletin & Review*, *20*(1), 54–72.

Lanier, M., Waddell, T. F., Elson, M., Tamul, D. J., Ivory, J. D., & Przybylski, A. (2019). Virtual reality check: Statistical power, reported results, and the validity of research on the psychology of virtual reality and immersive environments. *Computers in Human Behavior*, *100*, 70–78.

Law, E. L. C., Brühlmann, F., & Mekler, E. D. (2018). Systematic review and validation of the game experience questionnaire (GEQ)—Implications for citation and reporting practice. *Proceedings of the 2018 annual symposium on computer-human interaction in play* (pp. 257–270).

Lefrak, M. (2022, March 14). *Want to smell in virtual reality? A Vermont-based startup has the technology.* https://www.wbur.org/news/2022/03/14/virtual-reality-smell-ovr-technology. Accessed on October 16, 2022.

Meißner, M., & Oll, J. (2019). The promise of eye-tracking methodology in organizational research: A taxonomy, review, and future avenues. *Organizational Research Methods*, *22*(2), 590–617.

Miron-Spektor, E., Bear, J., & Eliav, E. (2022). Think funny, think female: The benefits of humor for women's influence in the digital age. *Academy of Management Discoveries*. https://doi.org/10.5465/amd.2021.0112

Mitchell, G. (2012). Revisiting truth or triviality: The external validity of research in the psychological laboratory. *Perspectives on Psychological Science*, *7*(2), 109–117.

Nesenbergs, K., Abolins, V., Ormanis, J., & Mednis, A. (2020). Use of augmented and virtual reality in remote higher education: A systematic umbrella review. *Education Sciences*, *11*(1), 8.

Neyret, S., Navarro, X., Beacco, A., Oliva, R., Bourdin, P., Valenzuela, J., Barberia, I., & Slater, M. (2020). An embodied perspective as a victim of sexual harassment in virtual reality reduces action conformity in a later Milgram obedience scenario. *Scientific Reports*, *10*(1).

Niu, M., & Lo, C. H. (2022). Do we see rendered surface materials differently in virtual reality? A psychophysics-based investigation. *Virtual Reality*, *26*(3), 1031–1045.

Oxley, J. A., Santa, K., Meyer, G., & Westgarth, C. (2022). A systematic scoping review of human-dog interactions in virtual and augmented reality: The use of virtual dog models and immersive equipment. *Frontiers in Virtual Reality*, *3*, 782023.

Pierce, C. A., & Aguinis, H. (1997). Using virtual reality technology in organizational behavior research. *Journal of Organizational Behavior*, *18*(5), 407–410.

Rizzo, A., Goodwin, G. J., De Vito, A. N., & Bell, J. D. (2021). Recent advances in virtual reality and psychology: Introduction to the special issue. *Translational Issues in Psychological Science*, *7*(3), 213–217.

Schubert, T., Friedmann, F., & Regenbrecht, H. (2001). The experience of presence: Factor analytic insights. *Presence: Teleoperators and Virtual Environments*, *10*(3), 266–281.

Serrano, B., Baños, R. M., & Botella, C. (2016). Virtual reality and stimulation of touch and smell for inducing relaxation: A randomized controlled trial. *Computers in Human Behavior*, *55*, 1–8.

Shorey, S., & Ng, E. D. (2021). The use of virtual reality simulation among nursing students and registered nurses: A systematic review. *Nurse Education Today*, *98*, 104662.

Somberg, G., (Ed.) (2021), *Game audio programming: Principles and practices* (Vol. 3). CRC Press.

Sterna, R., Siry, A. M., Pilarczyk, J., & Kuniecki, M. J. (2021). Psychophysiology in studying VR-mediated interactions: Panacea or a trick? Valuable applications, limitations, and future directions. *Frontiers in Virtual Reality*, *2*.

Stevenson, R., Josefy, M., McMullen, J. S., & Shepherd, D. (2020). Organizational and management theorizing using experiment-based entrepreneurship research: Covered terrain and new frontiers. *The Academy of Management Annals*, *14*(2), 759–796.

Teixeira, J., & Palmisano, S. (2021). Effects of dynamic field-of-view restriction on cybersickness and presence in HMD-based virtual reality. *Virtual Reality*, *25*(2), 433–445.

Wang, Y., Hu, Y., & Chen, Y. (2021). An experimental investigation of menu selection for immersive virtual environments: Fixed versus handheld menus. *Virtual Reality*, *25*(2).

Yaremych, H. E., & Persky, S. (2019). Tracing physical behavior in virtual reality: A narrative review of applications to social psychology. *Journal of Experimental Social Psychology*, *85*, 103845.

Zimmer, P., Buttlar, B., Halbeisen, G., Walther, E., & Domes, G. (2019). Virtually stressed? A refined virtual reality adaptation of the Trier Social Stress Test (TSST) induces robust endocrine responses. *Psychoneuroendocrinology*, *101*, 186–192.

A QUALITATIVE RESEARCHER'S JOURNEY: AN INTERVIEW WITH PROFESSOR DEAN A. SHEPHERD, PAULA O'KANE, AND SOTIRIOS PAROUTIS

Paula O'Kane[a], John R. Busenbark[b], Aaron F. McKenny[c] and Sotirios Paroutis[d]

[a]*University of Otago, New Zealand*
[b]*University of Notre Dame, USA*
[c]*Indiana University Bloomington, USA*
[d]*University of Warwick, UK*

ABSTRACT

In this chapter, Professor Dean Shepherd shares his experiences of becoming a qualitative researcher, bringing us on a [often personal] journey through his research beginnings, how his career developed and how he gravitated towards qualitative research. There are many lessons for Ph.D. students and early career academics and interesting takes on thinking about your research approach and impact.

Keywords: Qualitative; reflective; diverse teams; transitions; relationships

INTRODUCTION

In the third of our interviews across the *Research Methodology in Strategy and Management* series Paula O'Kane and Sotirios Paroutis talk with Professor Dean Shepherd about his experiences of being a qualitative researcher, what he has learned from these and what advice he can offer others. Professor Shepherd provided us with

Delving Deep
Research Methodology in Strategy and Management, Volume 15, 85–94
Copyright © 2025 Paula O'Kane, John R. Busenbark, Aaron F. McKenny and Sotirios Paroutis
Published under exclusive licence by Emerald Publishing Limited
ISSN: 1479-8387/doi:10.1108/S1479-838720240000015005

a very personal account of his journey, which brought his stories to life and enabled us to reflect upon our own careers.

We both drew the following highlights from the interview:

- Risk-taking: be prepared to choose new research topics and expand your methodological approaches as your academic career develops.
- Learning from doctoral students: be open with, and learn from, the individual journeys of doctoral students and plot ways to examine new issues using novel perspectives.
- "Me-search" and "We-search": be reflective of your life experiences and how they shape you as a researcher and the choices you make in terms of topics and methods.
- Impact: develop a deep appreciation of how research can make a difference to a research team, the study participants and the wider set of stakeholders that the research impacts upon.
- Team research: appreciate how to make the most of diverse research teams that enable us to push our understanding of a phenomenon.

FROM QUANTATIVE BEGINNINGS

I completed my Ph.D. at Bond University in Australia. I was the second Ph.D. graduate from the University, with the first being Keith Duncan, who is now a Professor of Accounting. He pursued conjoint studies which is common practice in accounting and auditing. Inspired by this, I decided to apply conjoint studies to the context of entrepreneurship. It seems logical to study entrepreneurship experts in a similar fashion.

I asked myself who the experts were and so decided to study the venture capitalists. I started off by looking at venture capitalists' assessments of entrepreneurs and their ventures. One of the reasons why I used conjoint analysis was that you use a much smaller sample size because its decisions nested within individuals. Then I realized there are so few venture capitalists in Australia that I had to pretty much get everybody. I travelled around State by State knocking on doors and eventually got enough to get started. So conjoint analysis was important for me. Although I started with venture capitalists, I was more interested in how entrepreneurs make their decisions about exploiting opportunities. This led me to working in decision-making, before adding cognition because it's related to decision-making.

TRANSITION POINT

While I was doing my doctoral program my father's business failed and caused us and the family a lot of distress and anxiety. When I felt that I was going to get tenure, I decided the time was right to write a paper about the grief of business failure, how it obstructs your ability to learn from failure and move on and how you need to have a process (Shepherd, 2003). It was a theory paper that I thought would never get published, but it got published in the *Academy of Management Review* (***I thought if I'm going to get rejected, I going to get rejected by the best!***).

That set the scene for further theory work and from there I started to transition to some more empirical work on failure. Some of my initial failure work was using surveys and conjoint analysis. As I proceeded along, I realized that I only really wanted to study quirky stuff, so I really wanted to push the boundaries of theories by only looking at things that were really, really interesting to me and highly risky, because I could now take those risks. *To answer, those sorts of questions required me to do inductive research*.

That transition started with Mike Haynie, a former doctoral student of mine at Syracuse, who was a lieutenant colonel in the Air Force. Mike set up a programme at Syracuse for veterans who were discharged from the military because of their injuries. He believed that while the Air Force trained them to be able to fight, they were not trained on how to come home (he's now the Vice President of Syracuse University). We studied the veterans at an entrepreneurship Boot Camp, and that was my first inductive study. *I had to teach myself how to do it.*

The research aimed to understand why some in the boot camp were able to use entrepreneurship as a vehicle to reestablish their identity and to move on with their lives, while others got stuck. We thought the only way that we could really understand it would be using some sort of inductive process. *And then from there, I really enjoyed that*. That paper was accepted in Journal of Applied Psychology, and I remember one of the reviewers saying, "JAP never publishes any papers about careers, it never paper publishes any inductive studies, but it should," and so they accepted it (Haynie & Shepherd, 2011). So that was quite lucky. From then on, I just wanted to *pursue really quirky research*, a little bit surprising and a little bit on the edges of knowledge, to push those knowledge boundaries. And so that's what I've been doing.

We mainly use semi-structured interviews, but we also collect newspapers and other data where we can. In India, and in South Africa, there isn't a lot of secondary sources of data, mainly because the people are semi-literate or illiterate and therefore don't have many records. Sometimes we find YouTube interviews. For example, if we're looking at illegal entrepreneurship there might be YouTube interviews with criminals that we can use as additional data.

I still do some field experiments. We did one recently where we looked at microcredit in Bangladesh exploring how women are more likely to start a venture if they hadn't been abused by their husbands, it's a terrible situation (Shahriar & Shepherd, 2019). We looked at the psychology to try to understand their entrepreneurial outcomes. Although they might get the money, their self-efficacy may be severely diminished by their home situation, by the patriarchal context.

RISK-TAKING

The first risk was when I wrote the paper on my dad and I wrote it because I believed, maybe overconfidently, I had tenure in the bag. *And so, tenure kind of gave me the confidence to be able to do that*. Developing the theory around failure helped to clarify my personal experiences, but at the time of the failure, I was a doctoral student so I just had to put it to the back of my mind thinking, "well, I can't possibly write about that now." It was about five years later I started to work on that paper. Since then, I've published about 15 papers on the topic and a couple of books, and so it really pushed it along.

Now, as a full professor, I'm only interested in doing stuff that interests me. I'm not really interested in building my CV or anything like that. I pursue things for intrinsic motivation reasons rather than extrinsic. Although you hope that's what you were doing all along, in the back of your mind you're thinking, "I've got to get this, and I've got to get it in here," and later on you don't have to worry. It's funny, *the more you don't worry about it the more you actually get it*.

More recently a friend of mine, Johan Wiklund, and I wrote a paper for *Entrepreneurship Theory and Practice* focusing on *"Me-Search," rather research* (Shepherd et al., 2021). To practice me-search you think about your life, the struggles you've had or things that have happened to you. You have idiosyncratic knowledge of it, and you're also motivated to pursue a solution to it, so it can provide a strong basis for interesting research. I use the concept when I am working with doctoral students. We start by talking about what their research direction is going be, by asking "who are you, what's your journey been like?" *I'm trying to find the "We-Search,"* where we connect, something that has some sort of personal resonance. With my current student, Sarah from South Africa, we are looking at the abalone industry as a sustainable venture in South Africa. This is something she can then go back and collect data on.

I always try and look towards something that's idiosyncratic in myself or in my co-authors. And I think that's how we got into doing quite a lot of research in India. I started working with Vinit Parida and Joakim Wincent. Vinit is in Sweden, but he's originally from India. We always sit together and think about problems that are occurring in India that we could study and that's led to a lot of interesting studies. *Some of them get published. Some of them don't.*

DOING QUALITATIVE RESEARCH IN INTERNATIONAL CONTEXTS

Entrepreneurship is common in the developing world, but it's uncommon in our publications because we study so much about what happens in the US or in the Western context. I think Howard Aldrich once told me "there are more studies on IPOs than there are IPOs." So that shows you where the focus is. Originally my data were from Australia, and the journals would always say "how does this generalize to the US?" One of my friends Julio Castro from Dominican Republic used to get outraged by that because he says, "if you publish with US data, they don't say, how is it generalizable?" And all I used to do is have one phrase which was something like "this may or may not generalize to other contexts." But I think now, *rather than being apologetic for our different context, you take it on full on and say, this is a feature of the paper.* It's partly a way of framing it, you highlight the importance of the phenomenon. If you can make the case that the phenomenon is extreme, then you can make the case that this is why you build theory. You build theory by pushing at the boundaries of the knowledge. Some reviewers may have a little bit of a bias against data that's not from where they're used to, but there is a way of telling a story that can help overcome some of that.

The great thing about working with Vinit and Joakim means I don't need to do the data collection. We sit together and bounce ideas off each other. Normally, I design the semi-structured interviews, they collect the data and then I'll do the analysis. There are challenges around data collection. For example, when you are in the slums of India or when you are exploring illegal entrepreneurship like the human trafficking of women. You can't collect data as a stranger, you have to be a local. So sometimes, we use local people that are part of that network, some are experts in data collection but others are not, but we use them to be able to collect the data. Mainly because the people are more willing to talk to them but also because they may not be very safe environments for us to go into. I said to Vinit and Joakim once, "what would it be like if we went into the slums?" And they said, "Oh, you should be right," but we said, "we want a better recommendation than should, we want to make sure we're 100% safe." I think we'd be safe. Although it's not ideal that I'm not the one collecting the data, when I get into the coding, I can really feel what's happening.

A lot of the research we did on adversity in India, and in Africa, we put into a book, made it open access and sent it to as many people in India as we knew. It was still an academic style book. I suppose that's always the quandary that we have. Do we go and spend more time having a practical impact, or do we keep going for a scholarly impact under the assumption that hopefully the scholarly impact trickles down. I suppose I'm more scholarly than directly going in and feeding that information back.

TRENDS IN QUALITATIVE RESEARCH

There's been a few trends in inductive research. I think one is towards greater acceptance. *Inductive research used to be done by non-Americans, and you would not see it as much in the journals.* Kathy Eisenhart was obviously an exception to that rule. Now inductive studies are becoming a lot more popular. In fact, I think for quite a long time the most impactful papers published in the *Academy of Management Journal* were inductive. There is a lot more acceptance of it, but I still had someone say to me, "you got that paper published, and you only have a sample size of 12," and I should have said to them, "you've published an *Academy of Management Review*, haven't you?" And they say "yes." And I should say "what was your sample size, it was zero, right?" When they say that it seems they're not understanding the method. You still get some reviewers asking you about generalizability where it's clear they don't understand the method itself.

For a while I thought we had a formula for doing it, but then some reviewers don't like the formula. There appears to be multiple camps, Eisenhart, Gioia and Langley and each address slightly different questions. *You should feel comfortable using one or the other depending on what your questions are.* Eisenhart is more a comparison between two groups of cases: Gioia is more all the cases together as a whole and Langley is more process and sequences of processes. That's just my very simple way of being able to categorize them. I've done mainly Eisenhart or Gioia, but then I also focus a lot on Michael Pratt's way. The Langley method is a little bit different, and so I haven't used that as much. If I had to pick where things were going to go in the future, I'd think that we're probably going to be doing more process research, more Langley-style research. I haven't really started to do that much myself. But I can see that trend. I think the reviewers don't like us having a formulaic research methods section. Some reviewers like the Gioia data structure and others don't want it in your paper and you never know which one to use. I don't know why they don't like it because we had that in deductive, empirical research. I think it would be good if we can come to some sort of agreement about what needs to be involved and what doesn't.

Another thing I've noticed, and I was almost going to write a paper about it, is the ***deductivisation of inductive research.*** When we first started doing it, you would not have a theoretical background section to your inductive study, which makes sense. The whole idea is that you have got this question, and you go in with a blank slate. And I think Eisenhart had a little bit to do with this, where she said, "no, it's all right to have a research question and your main constructs," which is useful. But now having a big theoretical background has become more of an expectation. The reviewers say, "you haven't fully taken in all the literature," and you go "well, that's not the purpose of an inductive study." So now they're starting to assess inductive methods with a deductive frame, and we've got some sort of hybrid happening. I think it's useful that we are all on the same page, so we're not getting people asking for completely different things. But I think it's a little bit of an awkward stage where we have a lot of deduction required for inductive studies. You can't write the theoretical background until you've discovered your model. It's a little bit backward. But some things we just have to accept. We can't change the world.

We're starting to look more outside the Western context. Particularly with entrepreneurship, where it's so important in those countries as it might be the only way that you ever get to feed your family. There was a stage a while back where everything had to be highly generalizable, every theory you came up with had to be some sort of grand theory, and now I think ***there's a trend towards having more contextualized theories.*** And we can have both, you can be more general or contextualized, but at least we are more open to being context specific.

As a journal editor, you want impactful papers, you want to increase your citations and so hopefully, the top journals can see that those can come from inductive studies. ***We need associate editors who are inductive researchers***, and we're now seeing those, at least at *Academy of Management Journal* and *Administrative Sciences Quarterly.* We also need reviewers who understand inductive, and as we start to see more people publishing inductive, we see a lot more reviewers. I would say, and I've heard other people say this as well, is that inductive researchers are like those insects that eat their young. Sometimes, they are too harsh in their reviews, and I don't know why that is. We can be our own worst enemies. Maybe it's because they got their paper rejected, and they are not going let your paper get through, and it becomes this whole thing where we don't let papers through. It's okay to be a bit tougher with comments but be a little bit easier with recommendations. Recommend a major revision rather than a reject and say, "look, if you can do this, and you can do this, and you can do this, well, then, maybe it's okay." A common joke amongst editors is that inductive research is very, very tough and maybe too tough. They should be focused more on the process of helping people improve the papers rather than just on the outcomes. There's no such thing as a perfect paper, but can they show some new insights and move the field forward? Maybe we need to change the goal posts a little bit.

Another trend is that they allow inductive studies to be longer papers. A lot of the journals now say you're an inductive study, here are an extra five pages or something like that. So at least, they realize that you need more space to communicate the paper.

COLLABORATORS

The first thing about collaboration for me is a simple rule, "would I have a beer with the person?" I wrote that in a book, and someone said, "but what if that person doesn't drink alcohol?," and I said, "you're missing the point, it's a simple rule, it just says this is a person I enjoy talking with, we're on the same page, I trust this person, and I enjoy working with them." It encapsulates a whole lot of things. *I don't work with anyone that I don't enjoy working with*, just because they might be able to help me get a paper published. I just don't think it's worth it for me. I enjoy the intrinsic part rather than worrying about the extrinsic part.

I would never have done any of the research in India if it wasn't for my collaboration with Vinit and Joakim. It was "we-search" again. The three of us sat down and enjoyed each other's company, so we said, "how are we going to work together, what could we do?" Then we started thinking about who each one of us is, and we focused on Vinit's Indian background and decided that was a unique context for different things, and then we just started exploring some of those ideas. Similarly, Mike Haynie's study on disabled veterans was devised because he was an Air Force Colonel, and he'd created the boot camp in the first place. Sarah, my current doctoral student, and I are trying to find the intersection between her interests and my interests. That's an important part of the creative process, trying to work out the topic. *I've chosen the person first and then come up with the topic.* Perhaps you can do it the other way around. You could choose a topic and go, okay, who can help me get access?

I've never really worked with a senior academic, it was just the way my Ph.D. happened. Then when I came to the US, I met Andrew Zacharakis who was the same year as me and we worked together. Maybe I missed some learning from not working with a senior co-author but *working with peers, you make all the mistakes together*. You learn everything together. You move forward together. People have different reasons for working with senior people or junior people. But I've always just kind of worked with my peers, and now I'm working with more junior people. When you're a senior person and you work with a junior person, you know how much it means to that person, and how excited they are by the process and that keeps you excited and energetic in the process as well. I have approached some senior people to work with me, Sarah Maitlis and Tom Lawrence on the rag pickers paper in the *Academy of Management Journal* (Shepherd et al., 2022). That was useful because I picked up little things that they do, that I don't do and that helps me keep learning as well.

ADVICE TO DOCTORAL STUDENTS

Definitely do "me-search." Think about who you are, what your path has been, what's your idiosyncratic thing and tap into that knowledge. Start to think about how this research fits within yourself. The way I communicate me-search to students is with examples from my own life, and I encourage them to do the same. Think about events in your life that were highly impactful, positive or negative, doesn't matter. For me it was my dad's business failing which inspired a lot of research on how to cope with business failure and learn from it. My Auntie Shirley's house got burned down when a firestorm hit Australia. Luckily, she was playing Bingo at the time otherwise she would have died. I started writing papers about how entrepreneurial ventures are created in the aftermath of disasters to help people overcome their suffering. So that's led to a stream of research on compassion venturing. When I was very young, my first girlfriend dumped me. I was devastated and reflecting on that, I wrote a paper about hitting Rock Bottom, and how hitting rock bottom can actually enable you to recover and build your identity. The one with my dad, I included my dad as part of the story that I told, but in the rock bottom paper I didn't. It was just the idea, but then it shifted direction, so it was like abductive research right where it just kind of pops up with this inquiry, and then you pursue it, and eventually, it looks like something completely different but stimulated by one of these "me/we-search" issues. We've all had highly impactful things that have helped or harmed us and each one of those could represent a research opportunity. When I'm sitting with a doctoral student, I try to understand who they are and what their journey has been, and together we can kind about what sort of research opportunities there might be.

The other thing is to say, there is no low-risk way of publishing in a high-quality journal. I see that research on my dad's business as high risk, but I think every paper that's going to get published in a top journal is probably high risk. *The biggest risk is not taking a risk to try and get published.* If it's connected to you, you're more motivated. I wish I'd taken bigger risks earlier; I wish I hadn't put off that paper about my dad for so long. I was working at getting publications, but I didn't even know I could publish. I was building my self-efficacy, basically, but I don't regret too much. *I think everything that's knocked me back has actually contributed to the journey.*

Enjoy the process because the outcomes are so far away. If you don't enjoy the process, you're not going to enjoy your whole career.

Work with other people because it's more fun. Don't work in too big a team, though. Once you've developed a relationship with a co-author keep it rolling, so you don't have a million co-authors that you're managing. You want to have key people that you know and trust, and you're friends with and you develop together.

This is not ideal but it reflects the practical realities. My doctoral students, though they will probably do an inductive study, will also do a deductive empirical study as part of their dissertation. The reason for that is that when you go and do a job talk it's very hard to present an inductive study, and it's way easier to present a deductive study. So, I think, even though people appreciate your published inductive studies, your working papers that are inductive are very difficult to present, particularly in, the time you have. I want them to be able to show that they have all those skills. I don't want them to focus in so much that they only do this or only do that. So, I encourage them to do inductive research because I think it really helps them tell a story and build theory, write good papers, understand the data and understand it deeply. But I also want them to get a good job and to be able to display that they have these empirical skills as well. I really like them to have both, not just focusing on one. Now, eventually, you might be able to focus on one, but at this stage, I think the practical realities are that you really need them to have both.

I wish I could have done my Ph.D. in the US, as things would have been different. But maybe things wouldn't have been different, or maybe things would have been worse. When your supervisors, for example, haven't published much research and you're trying to learn from them it's difficult but the fact that you got through situates you very well eventually, if you make it through the gauntlet. But a lot of people don't make it through and that's the problem. I suppose I had more of adversity in my Ph.D. program that having survived that it actually situated me really well, for when I came to the US to hopefully achieve success. I don't reflect back and wish I'd done things that differently.

NEXT PROJECT

We have been talking with Vinit about a paper on the child bride industry, but in the end, it was going to be too tough to collect the data. In the meantime, Vinit sent us a picture of him when he got married in India, and I said, "Oh, you look really young," and I was just joking that he was a child bride. But what had happened was that the photographer had colored his skin to make it look lighter, and making your skin lighter is a whole industry in India and other countries. Then I sent them a picture recently where I had a skin cancer cut out of my face and said, "well, that's the consequence of the other, white people often try to look darker." Now we're collecting data in India about people changing their color. It's got to do with caste system, so if you're lighter in India it means you're of a higher cast. We don't yet know what it's going to turn out to be, but it's some sort of identity story. But the worst thing is that some of these products are very, very detrimental to your health, it's like seriously bleaching your skin. ***So from inductive research, we don't know what we're going to find, but it's interesting*** that there are these all these businesses associated with changing people's skin color to suit their desired identity. The data is almost collected on that, so I'm looking forward to that.

REFERENCES

Haynie, J. M., & Shepherd, D. (2011). Toward a theory of discontinuous career transition: Investigating career transitions necessitated by traumatic life events. *Journal of Applied Psychology*, *96*(3), 501.

Shahriar, A. Z. M., & Shepherd, D. A. (2019). Violence against women and new venture initiation with microcredit: Self-efficacy, fear of failure, and disaster experiences. *Journal of Business Venturing*, *34*(6), 105945.

Shepherd, D. A. (2003). Learning from business failure: Propositions of grief recovery for the self-employed. *Academy of Management Review*, *28*(2), 318–328.

Shepherd, D. A., Maitlis, S., Parida, V., Wincent, J., & Lawrence, T. B. (2022). Intersectionality in intractable dirty work: How Mumbai ragpickers make meaning of their work and lives. *Academy of Management Journal*, *65*(5), 1680–1708.

Shepherd, D. A., Wiklund, J., & Dimov, D. (2021). Envisioning entrepreneurship's future: Introducing me-search and research agendas. *Entrepreneurship Theory and Practice*, *45*(5), 955–966.

EXECUTIVE PERSONALITY ASSESSMENT WITH LARGE LANGUAGE MODELS: UPDATING AN EXISTING TOOL AND ADVANCING SIMILAR MEASURES IN STRATEGY AND MANAGEMENT RESEARCH

Joseph S. Harrison[a], Steven Boivie[b], Timothy D. Hubbard[c] and Oleg V. Petrenko[d]

[a]*University of Tennessee at Knoxville, USA*
[b]*Texas A&M University, USA*
[c]*University of Notre Dame, USA*
[d]*University of Arkansas, USA*

ABSTRACT

This chapter describes the redevelopment of the Open Language Chief Executive Personality Tool (OLCPT), a language-based machine learning (ML) tool for assessing executives' traits along the five factor model (FFM) of personality (openness to experience, conscientiousness, extraversion, agreeableness, and neuroticism). Whereas the initial release of the OLCPT demonstrated the viability of using supervised machine learning to unobtrusively assess executives' personality traits, recent advances in artificial intelligence (AI) related to large language models (LLMs) warranted revisiting its development. After applying LLM embeddings and performing other updates, including expanding the training sample, the redeveloped tool (available at https://zenodo.org/records/10800801) achieved substantially higher convergent validity than the initial release. The updated tool also

Delving Deep
Research Methodology in Strategy and Management, Volume 15, 95–122
Copyright © 2025 Joseph S. Harrison, Steven Boivie, Timothy D. Hubbard and Oleg V. Petrenko
Published under exclusive licence by Emerald Publishing Limited
ISSN: 1479-8387/doi:10.1108/S1479-838720240000015006

demonstrates strong discriminant validity and reliability, and it can measure traits not included in the initial version (narcissism and humility). These improvements demonstrate the potential value of continuously updating existing, computer-aided measures in strategy and management research. Yet, such efforts may not always be feasible or even necessary. Thus, we also use this chapter to offer guidelines for determining when updating similar measures is worthwhile, urging scholars to carefully consider how existing tools perform and the relevance of advancements to the technologies underlying them. We conclude with additional suggestions for advancing measurement in our field, including keeping up with emerging technologies, encouraging complementary approaches to enable triangulation, avoiding the use of advanced techniques without carefully considering their applicability in a given context, and being realistic about what we ask for during the review process and what we consider a meaningful contribution in our field.

Keywords: Executive personality assessment; large language models (LLMs); generative pretrained transformers (GPTs); five factor model (FFM) of personality; narcissism; humility

When you can measure what you are speaking about, and express it in numbers, you know something about it; but when you cannot measure it, when you cannot express it in numbers, your knowledge is of a meagre and unsatisfactory kind. Kelvin (1883)

INTRODUCTION

Measurement is a critical aspect of strategy and management research, providing "an important foundation, grounding, and structure for theory development" (Gruber & Bliese, 2024, p. 1). As methods and measurement advance in our field, so too does our ability to develop and accurately test theory. This idea is perhaps no more evident than in research that has sought to develop theory on executives' underlying personalities. Early work in this area often relied on executives' demographic characteristics as proxies for their dispositional tendencies (see Carpenter et al., 2004). But understanding the need for more accurate and valid measures, later work drew directly from psychology research by applying psychometrically validated survey instruments to assess CEOs' personality traits, particularly those contained in the Five Factor Model (FFM) of personality (openness to experience, conscientiousness, extraversion, agreeableness, and neuroticism) (e.g., Colbert et al., 2014; Herrmann & Nadkarni, 2014; Nadkarni & Herrmann, 2010). Unfortunately, difficulties accessing CEOs for this purpose limited both the number and sample sizes of these studies. To address this, Harrison et al. (2019) used a mix of videometric and machine learning (ML) methods to develop a linguistic tool to unobtrusively assess CEOs' FFM traits from transcripts of their speech. The tool was subsequently applied in other large-scale studies to explore the role of CEO personality in market perceptions of risk and shareholder returns (Harrison et al., 2020), geographic dispersion and value creation in acquisitions (Aabo, Hanousek, et al., 2023; Aabo, Hansen, et al., 2023), monitoring by analysts (Andrei et al., 2024), and financial structuring decisions (Harrison & Malhotra, 2023).

Although this language-based tool was a major advance in unobtrusively measuring executives' personality traits, the Open Language Chief Executive Personality Tool (OLCPT) and similar measures recently introduced in strategy and management research (e.g., Choi et al., 2021; Hyde et al., 2024; Miric et al., 2023) bring with them a critical dilemma for scholars in our field. On the one hand, there is an eagerness to apply these novel measures to a myriad of research questions to broaden our understanding of organizations. On the other hand, there is a pressing need to rigorously evaluate the quality, validity, and reliability of these measures. This often involves re-examining and updating previously developed measures to ensure they are as robust as possible. In science, true progress is not about blindly adopting new techniques, it is about continually revisiting and refining our methods and theories to gain a more accurate understanding of the phenomena we examine. This chapter is driven by that ethos of continual improvement. We consider how an update to the OLCPT may be useful for scholars studying executive personality directly, and also as an example and guide for considering when improving similar measures may be worthwhile.

The decision to redevelop the OLCPT was inspired by recent advances in artificial intelligence (AI) related to large language models (LLMs). LLMs are a broad class of models that are pretrained on massive amounts of language data from the internet, which can then be fine-tuned to user-specific data for a variety of natural language processing (NLP) tasks, from text classification to sentiment analysis to text generation. Notably, this latter application is what has drawn recent and significant attention from industry and academia, as OpenAI's wide release of the web-based ChatGPT tool and its underlying Generative Pretrained Transformer (GPT) architecture have brought LLMs to the forefront of the AI revolution (Marr, 2023). In our case, the availability of the GPT model through OpenAIs application programmer interface (API) presented an opportunity to update the OLCPT and to improve its ability to accurately assess executive personality. Updating the tool also afforded us the opportunity to revisit other aspects of its development, including bolstering the training sample and revising other features that may have been limiting its prior performance. Consistent with expectations, applying OpenAI's GPT model and expanding the training sample substantially improved the tool's ability to assess executives' FFM personality traits. The updated tool is also able to unobtrusively measure two additional personality traits that have drawn considerable interest from strategic leadership scholars in recent years – narcissism and humility (e.g., Nie et al., 2022; Petrenko et al., 2019; Tang et al., 2018; Zhang et al., 2017; Zhu & Chen, 2015). Thus, the redeveloped tool holds promise in continuing to advance our understanding of executive's underlying traits.

Redeveloping the OLCPT also illustrates the potential value of continuously updating existing measures in strategy and management research, especially those based on AI, ML, and other computer-aided techniques. Yet, scholars are often torn between the precision gained from updates and the practical challenges they pose. For instance, many strategy and management scholars may not be trained in the latest ML techniques, despite the increasing availability of validated measures based in these techniques (e.g., Choi et al., 2021; Harrison et al., 2023; Hyde et al., 2023, 2024; Miric et al., 2023). Moreover, continuously updating measures with every technological advance may not be practical or efficient, considering the pace at which AI and ML evolve. Thus, after describing our reasoning and approach to redevelop the OLCPT, we offer recommendations to guide scholars in making informed decisions about when and how to make updates to their own measurement tools. We organize these guidelines around a set of questions that ask authors, as well as editors and reviewers, to consider how well an existing tool performs, how suitable it is for a given setting or application, and how relevant any recent technological advances may be for improving it. We conclude with additional, high-level recommendations to support continuous improvement of measurement in our field, particularly when applying computer-aided techniques related to AI and ML.

INITIAL DEVELOPMENT OF THE OLCPT (VERSION 1.5)

The first release of the OLCPT (version 1.5)[1] was developed in R using supervised ML and a training sample of 207 CEOs of S&P 500 companies. At a general level, supervised ML involves training a model to generalize patterns and relationships from labeled inputs (i.e., the training data), which can then be used to make predictions from new, unseen data. The training data for OLCPT 1.5 included psychometrically validated measures of the FFM traits from videometric analysis of 207 CEOs by Hill, Petrenko, and colleagues (Hill et al., 2019; Petrenko et al., 2016) as well as matched texts of those CEOs' speech during the question-and-answer (Q&A) section of earnings calls. Here, we summarize the steps that were followed to develop OLCPT 1.5 in order to briefly orient readers to both the videometric and ML approaches that were used. In the next section, we then detail recent advances in AI and LLMs that suggested the need to revisit the tool's development.

Videometric Assessment of CEO Personality

As described by Hill et al. (2019), videometric approaches involve "us[ing] third party ratings of video samples to assess individuals' characteristics with psychometrically validated instruments of the measures of interest." To assess CEO's personality traits, Hill, Petrenko, and colleagues (Hill et al., 2019; Petrenko et al., 2016) began by collecting publicly available videos of CEOs from online sources such as YouTube, Bloomberg, and CNBC. They selected videos that showed the CEOs in interviews or speeches where they expressed their views and opinions on various topics related to their firms and industries. They avoided videos that contained potentially biasing information such as the CEO's name, title, firm name, or firm performance. Next, they edited the videos to obtain segments of approximately 2 minutes and 30 seconds in length, which was determined to be the optimal length for valid measurement based on a pilot study (Petrenko et al., 2016). They also ensured that the video segments did not include any other individuals or distractions that could interfere with raters' focus on the CEO.

After collecting and editing video segments, the authors recruited doctoral students in psychology with experience in personality assessment to serve as raters. The raters were blind to the study hypotheses and the identities of the CEOs. They were offered a monetary incentive to participate in the study and used the well-validated 50-item International Personality Item Pool (Goldberg, 2000) to assess the FFM traits of the CEOs on a 7-point Likert scale. The authors trained the raters on the rating scale and procedures by using three example videos and discussing their observations with them. Video segments were randomly assigned to the raters, who were asked to complete the ratings in individual sessions across 2 months. Sessions were limited to no more than 1 hour to avoid rater exhaustion and to ensure rating independence. Each CEO was scored by three separate raters and the authors averaged those ratings to obtain the final videometric personality scores for the CEOs.

The International Personality Item Pool (IPIP) demonstrated strong reliability in the video sample, as evidenced by high alpha coefficients for each trait ($\alpha >$ 0.90). Alpha coefficients assess the extent to which items in a rating scale consistently measure the same underlying construct. A value above 0.9 indicates that the items in the scale are highly correlated and consistently measure the FFM traits. The raters also showed considerable agreement on their ratings, as indicated by average values for intraclass correlations (ICCs) of 0.54 (1, 3) and rating within-group agreement (r_{wg}) of 0.85. These metrics assess different aspects of agreement, with the former providing insights into the overall consistency and agreement of ratings made by different raters and the latter indicating the level of within-group agreement of ratings made by multiple raters. Both metrics range from 0 to 1 with higher values indicating greater consistency or agreement. An ICC above 0.5 suggests moderate overall consistency or agreement among raters and a r_{wg} of 0.85 suggests strong within-group agreement among raters.

Application of ML to Develop OLCPT 1.5

Using texts from the Q&A section of approximately 7,000 earnings calls for the same set of 207 CEOs, and the videometric scores from Hill, Petrenko, and colleagues as labels, Harrison et al. (2019) employed a three-stage process to develop OLCPT 1.5. The process included text vectorization, training and model selection, and trait prediction.

Text vectorization is a crucial step in NLP that transforms text data into numerical vectors, also referred to as embeddings or text representations. This is necessary because computers are unable to interpret raw text directly. They require numerical input. Vectorization converts text into numerical embeddings that algorithms can comprehend and analyze effectively. It also reduces the high-dimensionality of text data into lower dimensional representations, making it computationally manageable while retaining essential information. For OLCPT 1.5, the authors utilized Word2Vec (Mikolov et al., 2013) to extract relevant language features from a larger text corpus of CEO speech in approximately 100,000 segments of earnings call transcripts. Word2Vec converts words into numerical vectors based on their context in the text such that semantically similar words are located more closely in the vector space. For the OLCPT, each unique word in the dataset was assigned a corresponding vector in a multidimensional space to capture linguistic nuances and patterns within the CEOs' speeches that could be used as inputs to train ML models to predict their FFM traits.

For model training and selection, Harrison et al.'s (2019) aim was to optimize models to accurately estimate CEOs' personality scores while maintaining the variance and correlation structures in the videometric dataset. The authors partitioned the dataset into a training set (80%) and a test set (20%) to develop and validate the tool. Each CEO's speech was also divided into multiple, equal-sized segments to bolster the training dataset. The authors then employed Extreme Gradient Boosting (XGBoost) (Chen & Guestrin, 2016) to train models to predict CEOs' FFM traits using the observed scores and texts included in the training set. XGBoost is one of several ML algorithms that can be used to optimize predictive accuracy in ML tasks, and it was identified as the best performing algorithm when testing different alternatives for OLCPT 1.5.[2] In general, the purpose of these algorithms is to discern patterns and relationships within data, enabling tasks such as classification, regression, clustering, and anomaly detection. XGBoost specifically works by iteratively training models, learning from and correcting mistakes of preceding models until its performance is optimized for the data provided.

After training models for each trait, the authors applied them to the text observations in the test set to predict values of each personality trait for each of those observations. They then followed prior ML-based personality tools (Mairesse et al., 2007; Park et al., 2015) to validate the tool by calculating convergent correlations between the predicted scores and the observed scores in the test set. Convergent correlations provide an indication of predictive accuracy of a ML model, which ranged from 0.62 to 0.67 for the various traits included in OLCPT 1.5. Given these are correlations, values closer to 1.0 would reflect better predictive accuracy or higher convergent validity. Thus, while the tool certainly left some room for improvement, it provided a viable way to unobtrusively assess executives' FFM traits and represented a substantial improvement over previous ML-based personality tools that achieved convergent correlations up to 0.35 (Mairesse et al., 2007) or 0.43 (Park et al., 2015). The tool also demonstrated strong discriminant validity and reliability (see Harrison et al., 2019, pp. 1,322–1,323) and the authors provided further evidence of its content validity in a follow-up study (see the Online Appendix of Harrison et al., 2020).

After training and validating the models, the authors applied them to the larger text corpus initially used to create the text embeddings in order to predict personality scores for all the CEOs in that broader sample. This allowed them to generate scores of the FFM personality traits for more than 3,000 CEOs of S&P 1500 firms. Other scholars also applied the tool to assess these traits for their own unique samples, and together, these measures provided the basis for the aforementioned studies exploring the effects of CEO personality on firm strategy, financial structure, and other organizational outcomes (Aabo, Hanousek, et al., 2023; Aabo, Hansen, et al., 2023; Andrei et al., 2024; Harrison et al., 2020; Harrison & Malhotra, 2023).

RECENT ADVANCEMENTS IN AI AND LLMS

Although OLCPT 1.5 proved useful in facilitating large-scale studies of CEO personality, recent advances in AI suggested the need to revisit the tool's development. In particular, embedding techniques based on LLMs have recently gained significant attention, especially following OpenAI's release of its ChatGPT-3 demo in 2022, which was built on the third generation of its GPT technology. Indeed, while the genesis of LLMs began as much as a decade ago with the introduction of advanced embedding techniques like Word2Vec, OpenAI's release of ChatGPT-3 was arguably the pivotal moment in their development that brought them to the forefront of the AI revolution and led to the recent surge in interest and use of LLMs across academia and industry.[3] It was also the impetus for us to revisit the development of the OLCPT. Thus, this section briefly describes LLMs and OpenAI's GPT model before outlining how we applied this new method to redevelop the OLCPT.

A Brief Background on LLMs

LLMs represent a broad class of extremely large, pretrained language models that aim to comprehend and generate human language. They utilize sophisticated learning methods to capture the contextual nuances, syntax, and semantics of text. This typically involves the use of deep learning techniques, which differ from standard ML in their ability to automatically learn intricate hierarchical representations from raw data. They accomplish this by leveraging multilevel neural network architectures that imitate the structure of the human brain and are capable of capturing complex patterns and dependencies across various levels of abstraction.

One such architecture that was particularly critical to the development of LLMs is the transformer architecture introduced by Vaswani et al. (2017). This architecture revolutionized AI-based NLP through its self-attention mechanism, which allows the model to weigh the importance of different words or tokens in a sequence and to capture dependencies between different positions in the sequence simultaneously. As a result of this mechanism, the transformer architecture can generate highly contextualized text embeddings, at scale, and in a highly efficient way. Following the introduction of the transformer architecture, multiple LLMs based on that architecture quickly emerged, including OpenAI's first generation GPT (Radford et al., 2018) and Google's Bidirectional Encoder Representations from Transformers (BERT) (Devlin et al., 2018) and Text-To-Text Transfer Transformer (T5) (Raffel et al., 2020).

Although each of these models was developed using different pretraining methods, a key feature of all of them is that they were built on vast amounts of diverse data. For example, GPT-1 was pretrained on an immense dataset of publicly available books, articles, and websites from the internet, and it included 117 million parameters, which reflect the weights and biases in the various layers and components of the neural network. Similarly, BERT was pretrained on a massive dataset including the BooksCorpus and the English portion of Wikipedia, and two different model sizes, respectively, comprising 110 million parameters (BERT-small) and 340 million parameters (BERT-large). Finally, T5 has four versions ranging from 60 million to about 3 billion parameters, each trained using a vast and diverse range of data for tasks framed as text-to-text conversion, including translation, summarization, and question answering.

For each of these language models, the vast amount of diverse data and extensive parameters used in the pretraining process, along with the transformer-based architecture, allow them to produce extremely rich and generalizable representations of language. The contextual understanding LLMs acquired during pretraining also enables them to be fine-tuned for specific tasks with minimal task-specific data. During fine-tuning, the selected model can be applied to users' text data to generate task-specific embeddings that effectively capture the semantic relationships between words. This makes LLMs highly versatile and applicable across a wide array of NLP tasks. All of these benefits increased exponentially following OpenAI's release of ChatGPT and its underlying GPT-3 architecture.

ChatGPT and OpenAI's GPT-3

OpenAI released ChatGPT in November 2022 and it quickly garnered widespread attention for its ability to generate human-like text in response to user-written prompts. At the core of its evolution was GPT-3, the third generation of OpenAI's GPT model. In general, GPTs function by applying a transformer-based architecture to predict the next word in a sentence, given the context of preceding words. This focus is somewhat different from other LLMs, for example, BERT, which focuses on understanding the bidirectional context of words in a sequence. But what truly set GPT-3 apart from other LLMs was its unprecedented scale. A massive improvement over previous LLMs, including earlier generations of the GPT model, GPT-3 boasted an extraordinary 175 billion parameters and was pretrained on a substantial portion of the internet. Its massive scale provided the basis for GPT-3's groundbreaking language generation capabilities, popularized through ChatGPT.

Besides vastly improving its language generation capabilities, GPT-3's unprecedented scale also improved the model's broader understanding of diverse linguistic patterns and contexts relative to other LLMs. Moreover, OpenAI democratized access to GPT-3 through its API.[4] The API enables developers and researchers to integrate advanced LLMs into various applications without the need for extensive ML infrastructure. Instead, users can access the API and apply OpenAI's GPT model to generate sample-specific embeddings that can be used for a wide range of downstream NLP tasks, including text classification, sentiment analysis, named entity recognition, and any other task where contextual understanding of the text is critical (Dale, 2021; Floridi & Chiriatti, 2020). To use its API, developers need only obtain an API key, after which they can make HTTP requests to OpenAI's servers and write script to programmatically handle the model's responses. The API's flexibility accommodates experimentation with various programming languages and frameworks, tailoring integrations to meet specific project requirements. As previously noted, the accessibility of OpenAI's GPT models through its API also provided the basis for our update to the OLCPT.

REDEVELOPMENT OF THE OLCPT (VERSION 2.0)

Again, OLCPT 1.5 was trained using embeddings that were based on a relatively small and unique text corpus. While the tool outperformed earlier ML-based personality measures, we expected that applying LLMs would allow us to generate richer embeddings that could lead to more accurate and generalizable predictions of CEOs' personality traits. Thus, we sought to refine the tool by integrating these advanced embedding techniques into its development. This exercise also provided an opportunity to revisit other aspects of the tool's development. Table 1 provides a summary of the methods used to develop the

Table 1. Training Method Comparison.

	OLCPT 1.5	OLCPT 2.0
Training Data		
Text corpus	7,245 total earnings calls	20,722 total earnings calls 5,269 CEO-year observations
Validated trait scores*	All FFM for 207 CEOs	Extraversion for 463 CEOs ($N = 3,641$) Other FFM for 328 CEOs ($N = 2,794$) Narcissism for 498 CEOs ($N = 4,326$) Humility for 237 CEOs ($N = 2,473$)
Model Development		
Programming language (architecture software)	R (R-studio)	Python (Jupyter lab)
Main libraries	H2O (Java); XGBoost	Scikit-learn; Gensim; PyCaret
Embedding technique	Word2Vec embeddings (Sample specific)	GPT embeddings from OpenAI's API (Fine-tuned to sample)
ML algorithm	Extreme Gradient Boosting Machines	K-Nearest Neighbors
Additional Dependencies		
Training models	Models simultaneously trained for all traits. Correlation structure of the training data was used as a dependency.	Models *independently* trained for each trait. Correlation structure of the training data was *not* used as a dependency.
Prediction models	Standardizes scores across the predicted sample.	No standardization applied to the predicted sample.

Note: The values of N provided in parentheses of the third column reflect the total number of annualized text observations attributed to the CEOs for which we had a validated score for each corresponding trait included in OLCPT 2.0.

final version of the current release, OLCPT 2.0, compared to those used to develop OLCPT 1.5. Below we describe the steps we took to develop the new version of the tool, highlighting relevant improvements as we go.

Training Data

Data used to redevelop the tool were similar to those of OLCPT 1.5, except that we expanded the size of the training sample to mitigate overfitting and improve the redeveloped tool's accuracy and generalizability. Overfitting can occur when an ML tool performs well on the training and test data but has limited generalizability in new data. The risk of overfitting is higher in smaller training samples because the model has fewer examples to learn from, making it more likely to capture noise or random fluctuations in the data and incorrectly interpret those as meaningful patterns. Expanding the training sample can help to alleviate this issue by providing more diverse examples for learning, reducing the likelihood that the model will misinterpret idiosyncrasies in those data as meaningful, generalizable patterns.

In comparison to OLCPT 1.5, which was trained using videometric scores for 207 CEOs from Hill et al. (2019) and corresponding text from about 7,000 earnings call transcripts (from Lexis Nexis' Full Disclosure Wire), the training data for OLCPT 2.0 included a more diverse set of observed scores for up to 2.4 times the number of CEOs (depending on the trait) and associated text from more than 20,000 total earnings call transcripts (from Capital IQ Transcripts). The observed personality scores were collected and validated in three separate data collection efforts, which were shared with us by three distinct coauthor teams. They included the same videometric FFM scores for the 207 CEOs from Hill et al. (2019), plus additional videometric data from those authors for narcissism ($N = 373$) and humility ($N = 239$), as well as videometric scores of narcissism and extraversion for 300 CEOs from Gupta et al. (2018) and historiometric FFM scores for 160 CEOs from Benischke et al. (2019).[5] Each of these samples was validated in a way similar to the videometric approach described previously.[6]

Combining these samples during the training process improved the predictive accuracies of our final models by up to 15% relative to models trained on any of these samples separately. This offers evidence that expanding the training sample increased the tool's validity and generalizability. Because the new data included scores for humility and narcissism, we were also able to train models for those additional traits. Overall, given some differences in the traits and CEOs included in the sourced subsamples, the number of scores used to train models for each trait varied from 239 at the low end (for humility) to 498 at the high end (for narcissism). Text from the Q&A section of the 20,722 earnings call transcripts were then matched to each CEO and aggregated on an annual basis to train new models for each trait. Table 1 specifies the numbers of unique CEOs and annualized text observations used to train models for each trait.

Model Development

After compiling the expanded dataset, we trained models to predict CEOs' personality traits from texts of their speech. We trained the new models in Python using the popular *Scikit-learn* and *Gensim* libraries. This represents another difference from OLCPT 1.5, which was trained in R using H2O, an ML library that runs on Java. We opted to use Python because of versioning issues with H2O and its dependence on Java, which prevented OLCPT 1.5 from running properly on some users' machines. In our experience, Python also tends to be more accessible to users than R, so this change should facilitate future use of the redeveloped tool.

We began the training procedure by loading the full annualized text data into Python (N = 5,269 CEO-year observations) and then applying and fine-tuning OpenAI's GPT model to those data. Again, doing so required us to obtain an API key and to include code in our training script to directly access the OpenAI servers via HTML request. This allowed us to apply their GPT model directly to our text corpus to generate robust text embeddings for our sample that could be used for the training task. We then imported the observed scores for the various personality traits in our sample and merged those with the GPT embeddings, creating separate data frames to be used to train models for each trait. Following best practice, and similar to Harrison et al. (2019), we also split each data frame into a training and validation set (80%) and a test set (20%) before developing models for a given trait.

After organizing and partitioning the data frame, we used *PyCaret* to train and validate models for each trait. *PyCaret* is a powerful, open-source library in Python designed to simplify and accelerate the ML workflow. Its streamlined functionality allows users to experiment with multiple ML algorithms, perform hyperparameter tuning, and compare model performance. Of particular note, *PyCaret* contains a comprehensive selection of ML algorithms across multiple categories that can be used for modeling. Because it is difficult to know a priori which algorithm will perform best for a given task, we allowed *PyCaret* to cycle through all relevant algorithms in the library, generating models for each, and then use grid search to identify the algorithm that optimized each model's performance.[7] As it happened, a single algorithm, K-Nearest Neighbors (KNN), performed best for all traits. KNN works by storing all available data points and their values and then calculating the Euclidian distance between each data point and all other points in the dataset. It then selects the K closest points (neighbors) based on distance and assigns a value based on averages of those points' values. The value of K in KNN represents the number of neighbors to consider. Our final models use the default value of K = 5 and apply uniform weights when averaging values.[8] The weighting structure was a learned parameter during model training.

As part of the training procedure, we also applied K-folds cross validation. This method supports more robust modeling by creating multiple splits within the training data and iterating through those splits while training the model. That is, it splits the data into K groups of approximately equal size, designating one as a validation set and using the remaining data to train the model. It then cycles through the data until each group has been used as a validation set once (Refaeilzadeh et al., 2009). Model parameters are updated and learned during each training phase. This method provides a more comprehensive understanding of how well a given model generalizes across different partitions of the dataset and helps mitigate potential issues of over-fitting or underfitting. In our case, we used the common split of $K = 10$ and calculated performance metrics as the mean of the metrics obtained from each fold after the 10 iterations of training and validation. To further validate each model, we then applied it to the test set – the 20% of the data that the machine did not see during the training procedure – and calculated convergent correlations by comparing predicted values from the model to the observed values in that validation set. We report these values in the model performance section.

Additional Dependencies

In redeveloping the tool, we not only integrated several new methods and procedures, but we also made important decisions about what not to include from the previous version. We removed two specific dependencies built into OLCPT 1.5 that were originally implemented to improve accuracy but ended up limiting the tool's generalizability. First, in the initial release, models for all FFM traits were developed simultaneously and the tool was designed to generate predictions that mirrored the correlation structure among those traits in the training data. While this increased the predictive accuracy of the tool in the original training and test sets, it led to inflated correlations among predicted values in new samples. This is likely because the initial set of training examples was overly constrained, so that forcing its correlation structure onto new data prevented the tool from accurately capturing the covariance in the new sample. Second, to ensure meaningful variance in its predictions, OLCPT 1.5 was designed to standardize predicted scores within the sample provided to the tool for trait prediction. While this approach produced reliable predictions for samples similar in size to the original sample that Harrison et al. (2019) used for their predictive test of the tool ($N = 3,449$ CEOs), it generated distorted and unreliable predictions in smaller samples. The redeveloped tool mitigates these issues by removing those constraints, allowing for independent training and subsequent trait prediction.

Model Performance

Table 2 provides metrics for the best performing models for each trait in OLCPT 2.0. As standard metrics for the training models, we used both mean absolute error (MAE) and mean squared error (MSE). Whereas MAE measures the average magnitude of errors between predicted and actual values, MSE is the average of the squared differences between those values. In general, lower MAE and MSE values indicate better model performance. However, "good" values of these error metrics depend on the scale of the predicted measure. In our case, the updated models produced MAEs between 0.2 and 0.32 (with an average of 0.25) and MSEs between 0.11 and 0.3 (with an average of 0.18). Given each personality trait is scored on a 7-point scale, MAE and MSE values in this range are very reasonable.

Table 2. Performance Metrics (OLCPT 2.0).

Personality Trait	MAE	MSE	Convergent Correlation
Openness	0.22	0.14	0.88
Conscientiousness	0.32	0.30	0.88
Extraversion	0.24	0.14	0.83
Agreeableness	0.23	0.17	0.82
Neuroticism	0.20	0.12	0.84
Narcissism	0.32	0.23	0.83
Humility	0.20	0.11	0.87
Min	0.20	0.11	0.82
Max	0.32	0.30	0.88
Mean	0.25	0.18	0.85

Because OLCPT 1.5 and other prior ML-based personality tools used convergent correlations as indicators of predictive accuracy or convergent validity, we also calculated these values in our test sample as a way to better gauge the relative performance of OLCPT 2.0. Table 3 provides the convergent validities for each model in OLCPT 2.0 compared to those of the final trained models for OLCPT 1.5. As shown in the table, the updated models achieved convergent correlations between 0.82 and 0.85. These values reflect increases of between 0.15 and 0.24 in the convergent correlations for OLCPT 2.0 relative to OLCPT 1.5, or between 22% and 38% improvement. Overall, the redeveloped version of the OLCPT outperforms the original version across each of the FFM traits. And again, the updated tool has the added benefit of measuring two additional traits – narcissism and humility. Such improvements illustrate the value of redeveloping the tool using an expanded training sample and more advanced embedding techniques.

Table 3. Convergent Correlation Comparison (OLCPT 1.5 versus OLCPT 2.0).

Personality Trait	OLCPT 1.5	OLCPT 2.0	Difference	Percent Improvement
Openness	0.67	0.88	0.21	32%
Conscientiousness	0.64	0.88	0.24	38%
Extraversion	0.65	0.83	0.18	28%
Agreeableness	0.67	0.82	0.15	22%
Neuroticism	0.62	0.84	0.22	36%
Narcissism	–	0.83	–	–
Humility	–	0.87	–	–
Min	0.62	0.82	0.15	22%
Max	0.67	0.88	0.24	38%
Mean	0.65	0.85	0.20	31%

Additional Validation

We also performed additional tests to further validate the redeveloped tool. To do so, we followed a similar approach as Harrison et al. (2019) by applying the new models to a broader sample of earnings call transcripts and exploring additional characteristics of the predicted values from those models. The sample for these tests included 2,013 unique CEOs of S&P 1500 firms between 2000 and 2015, with transcripts for these CEOs taken from Capital IQ Transcripts. The associated text corpus included text spoken by these CEOs in the Q&A section of the calls on an annual basis, for a total of 7,493 CEO-year observations.

Using this sample, we looked for evidence of discriminant validity by comparing intercorrelations among the predicted values of the CEOs' traits from the new models to those in the training sample. Table 4 presents these intercorrelations, with

Table 4. Trait Intercorrelations.

	Training	Prediction
FFM Traits		
Openness-Conscientiousness	0.77	0.77
Openness-Extraversion	0.51	0.25
Openness-Agreeableness	−0.03	−0.10
Openness-Neuroticism	0.23	0.34
Conscientiousness-Extraversion	0.52	0.30
Conscientiousness-Agreeableness	−0.15	−0.27
Conscientiousness-Neuroticism	0.27	0.40
Extraversion-Agreeableness	−0.01	0.03
Extraversion-Neuroticism	−0.19	−0.20
Agreeableness-Neuroticism	−0.55	−0.65
abs(Min)	0.01	0.03
abs(Max)	0.77	0.77
abs(Mean)	0.32	0.33
N	328	7,493
Narcissism and Humility (with FFM)		
Narcissism-Humility	−0.22	−0.08
Narcissism-Openness	0.04	0.06
Narcissism-Conscientiousness	0.02	0.10
Narcissism-Extraversion	0.31	0.13
Narcissism-Agreeableness	−0.26	−0.08
Narcissism-Neuroticism	−0.15	0.01
Humility-Openness	0.10	0.02
Humility-Conscientiousness	0.04	−0.13
Humility-Extraversion	0.03	0.06
Humility-Agreeableness	0.15	0.17
Humility-Neuroticism	−0.14	−0.17
abs(Min)	0.02	0.01
abs(Max)	0.31	0.17
abs(Mean)	0.13	0.09
N	62 to 233	7,493

values among the FFM traits in the top panel and values with narcissism and humility in the bottom panel. Intercorrelations among the predicted values follow similar patterns as those in the training sample, both in terms of direction and magnitude, with most of these either at or below the levels found in the training sample. Among the FFM traits, the average intercorrelations for the predicted scores are |0.33|, compared to |0.32| for the training sample. Similarly, average intercorrelations with narcissism and humility are |0.09|, compared to |0.13| in the training sample. These values not only provide further evidence of the accuracy of the new models, but also demonstrate that they are at least as effective at discriminating between traits as the psychometrically validated instruments used to score the training data. This provides evidence of the discriminant validity of the redeveloped models.

We also assessed the internal consistency of the redeveloped tool by calculating ICCs for predicted values of each trait for the same CEOs across different years. We used a subset of 1,031 CEOs from the broader sample who had at least 1,000 words across three separate years. ICCs for each trait are provided in Table 5 and ranged from 0.78 to 0.86 with an average of 0.83. These values reflect moderate to strong internal consistency for the redeveloped models, while also demonstrating some variance in how CEOs express their personalities over time. The latter finding suggests an additional benefit of the tool, in that OLCPT 1.5 pooled text across years, whereas users can possibly use OLCPT 2.0 to assess personality on an annual basis to consider slight variations in how executives express their personalities in different situations or across time.

Limitations and Future Development

Despite the improvements, we acknowledge that OLCPT 2.0 still has some limitations, some of which represent opportunities for future development. One inherent challenge with using pretrained LLMs from an API is that, while those models provide rich embeddings because of their extremely large training sets,

Table 5. Intraclass Correlations.

	ICC
Openness	0.85
Conscientiousness	0.83
Extraversion	0.78
Agreeableness	0.86
Neuroticism	0.86
Narcissism	0.78
Humility	0.83
Min	0.78
Max	0.86
Mean	0.83

their development and underlying structure remain somewhat of a black box to scholars. We can apply the models using available APIs, but the full underlying code and algorithms are generally proprietary and are not shared outside the companies that develop them. One consequence of this is that we are unable to generate or assess interpretability metrics for our tool (e.g., feature importance, saliency maps, etc.) (Carvalho et al., 2019; Gilpin et al., 2018), which would be possible if we applied deep learning techniques to generated sample-specific embeddings, rather than fine-tuning OpenAI's GPT model to generate embeddings. In our case, this was a tradeoff we were willing to make to improve the accuracy and generalizability of the tool. But future scholars may consider whether they want to rely on pretrained LLMs and existing APIs when building or developing new measures. In cases where scholars opt to create their tools completely from scratch, they may also consider applying interpretability metrics to enhance trust and adoption of their tools (Gilpin et al., 2018).

Another limitation of the tool is that the token length for OpenAI's GPT available through the API is currently limited to 8,100 words or tokens, due to the high complexity and computational demands of its transformer-based architecture. In our experience developing tools for personality assessment, we have found that the minimum token length needed to generate reliable personality scores is about 1,000, so this limitation does not appear to be a problem in our context. However, it is still possible that when using the API, it will involve cutting off some relevant information. One possible workaround would be to split up bodies of text that are larger than the 8,100 token limit and then enter them in ways that are below the upper limit (e.g., by averaging or, in our case, predicting values on an annual basis). However, scholars who are considering the development of other tools could consider long-range transformers (Tay et al., 2020), which may not have these same token limitations.

We will also note that our training data inherently have some dependencies. This is especially true because we have text from the same individuals over multiple years. Again, this decision was made to bolster the training sample, because small samples tend to constrain the overall robustness and performance of ML-based tools. However, these dependencies could also affect subsequent training and the ultimate structure and parameters included in the final trained models. In the future, we or other scholars may experiment with methods to model this dependency to further improve the accuracy and generalizability of the OLCPT and similar tools.

Finally, it is important to note what the generated scores from the tool do and do not represent, and how they should be used and interpreted. Given the data and methods used to train the tool, its output reflects an estimate of the observed personality traits of the target subject based on how they express themselves in their language use. Thus, the scores most closely resemble what the personality literature refers to as "observer scores" or "other ratings" rather than "self-ratings" or one's "true" personality (Connelly & Ones, 2010; Funder, 1980; Letzring et al., 2005). We expect this will not inhibit future use of the tool to a great extent because most scholars are likely to be interested in studying variation in executives' observed personalities as expressed in the context of their executive roles, which we believe the tool captures. However, scholars should be careful not to extrapolate their interpretations beyond this (e.g., as executives' "true" personalities, how they would describe themselves, or how they express themselves in their personal lives). Moreover, given most users are likely to use the tool's output in down-the-line empirical models, they should consider statistical techniques that can minimize the effect of potential measurement error from the use of generated measures (Yang et al., 2018).

Future Use of the OLCPT

The redeveloped tool is available for future use on the Zenodo platform, at https://zenodo.org/records/10800801. The downloads include a ReadMe file for installation and use, as well as a guide for citing the correct version of the tool. One important note is that, because the GPT models use OpenAI's API, users will need to set up a personalized API key and load their account with funds to apply those models to their own text data. The cost to generate embeddings from OpenAI's API should be small for most samples. For example, the cost to score our larger sample of more than 7,000 observations was between $4 and $5 (USD).

We may also continue to update the tool occasionally as the need arises or as additional advances in its underlying technologies become available. To benefit from these updates, users should ensure they are using the most recent version of the tool. Zenodo makes it easy to track these updates by providing a notification and link to the most up-to-date version when accessing earlier versions. As scholars apply the updated OLCPT, they would ideally cite both this chapter and the original paper developing the tool to demonstrate how it has evolved over time. Users may also consider citing other studies that have applied the tool as evidence of its utility and predictive validity.

GUIDELINES FOR USING AND UPDATING COMPUTER-AIDED MEASURES

The forgoing exercise demonstrates the value of updating the OLCPT to take advantage of major advances in its underlying technologies. Yet, scholars may often be uncertain about when it is necessary or useful to update other existing tools or measures. We develop guidelines in this regard, using a set of questions we believe can help scholars, as well as editors and reviewers, balance between pragmatism and relying on existing tools with continual improvement and advancing the science of strategy and management.

Question 1: How Well Does the Current Tool Perform?

Evaluating the performance of an existing measure, particularly in the context of advanced technologies like ML, necessitates a deep understanding of its capabilities and limitations. Here, it is important to acknowledge that no tool can achieve perfection. The inherent complexity of the constructs and data that we consider in strategy and management research set a fundamental limit on their precision (Hyde et al., 2023). Even ML techniques, despite their advanced capabilities, can only approximate the underlying patterns within these complex data, leading to inherent limitations in their accuracy and reliability. Thus, when assessing the usefulness of a particular tool, a pragmatic approach is advisable. This approach should hinge on the tool's validity and its comparative performance against previous methods. Validity in this context refers to the extent to which the tool accurately measures or predicts the intended construct. If the tool demonstrates a reasonable level of validity and marks an improvement over prior measures, we believe that it is generally worthwhile to continue using it. This perspective aligns with the principle of incremental progress in technology and data analysis, where each new version of a tool or method builds upon the limitations of the last.

The OLCPT illustrates this point effectively. As previously noted, the initial version of the tool achieved convergent correlations between 0.6 and 0.7, which left room for additional improvement, but indicated substantially better predictive accuracy than earlier ML-based personality tools that produced convergent correlations in the range of 0.2–0.4. It was also more suited for application to executive samples than previous measures because it was developed and validated specifically on a sample of CEOs of major companies, whereas its predecessors were developed using data from psychology students, Twitter users, and other disparate samples. This, along with the increased accuracy and validity of OLCPT 1.5, provided a strong basis for the previously cited large-scale studies on CEO personality. Of course, more recent advances in LLMs provided an opportunity to further improve the tool's accuracy. However, that opportunity does not negate the fact that the initial release was a substantial improvement over previous methods, and a useful basis for the studies that applied it. Moving forward, the same can be said of OLCPT 2.0. While it too has certain limitations, which we have tried to make transparent, we believe it represents a major advance in executive personality measurement, and that it can be confidently applied in future studies to continue advancing our understanding of executive personality, so long as it is applied correctly.

Overall, it is important for our field to maintain a realistic view regarding the capabilities of the measurement tools we apply. Though striving for perfection is admirable, we should prioritize progress over perfection. This pragmatic view encourages the ongoing use and development of tools like the OLCPT, recognizing their value in advancing our understanding and analysis of complex organizational phenomena, while also being transparent about their limitations and potential areas for future development.

Question 2: What Are Recent Advancements that Would Be Relevant for the Tool?

The prior points notwithstanding, it is also advisable for strategy and management scholars to keep track of ongoing improvements in the technologies underlying existing tools that may suggest the need or value of revisiting their development. Continual advancements in the field of computer science are particularly pertinent to the development and optimization of the measurement tools we tend to apply in our field. Two critical features of these advancements we suggest scholars should consider when applying a pragmatic approach to continuous improvement are their scale and their applicability to a given measurement tool.

The scale of the advancement. In general, developments in the computer sciences can be categorized as either incremental improvements or major advancements, and these have different implications for our pragmatic approach to continuously improving measurement in strategy and management research. In the first case, minor adjustments and refinements to existing methods are a constant phenomenon. So, while occasionally revisiting such incremental improvements can certainly be beneficial, it is important to acknowledge the practical challenges of keeping pace with minor updates. Moreover, the likelihood that any given incremental improvement will substantially enhance the performance of a tool is relatively low. In the computer sciences, minor modifications often aim at optimization and efficiency (such as improving the ease of calculation or decreased power usage) rather than groundbreaking changes in functionality or capability (e.g., Deng et al., 2021; Hashimoto et al., 2015; Li et al., 2018). Thus, our recommendation is that those who develop measurement tools for strategy and management research periodically revisit the underlying technologies to ensure that a tool adequately captures relevant improvements. But such updates should not be a prerequisite to continue applying an existing tool in our field, particularly if it has been well validated.

In contrast to incremental improvements, major advancements in the computer sciences are pivotal moments that necessitate a reevaluation of existing measurement tools. The release of OpenAI's GPT-3, for instance, represented a substantial leap in the capabilities of LLMs with potential application to innumerable NLP tasks. Such advancements signal the need for strategy and management scholars to test new methods and potentially integrate them into existing measurement tools. For the OLCPT, the emergence of GPT-3 prompted us to explore how LLMs could enhance the tool, given the prior version relied on sample-specific embeddings. Consistent with this, we encourage strategy and management scholars to keep track of major advancements in the computer sciences and related fields to understand when it may be necessary to revisit and update existing measurement tools.

The applicability of the advancement. It is also important to understand that not all advancements in computer science will uniformly benefit all measurement tools. The decision to incorporate a new development should be driven by its relevance and potential impact on the specific tool. This approach involves judiciously testing new methods to assess their compatibility and efficacy. It is important for scholars and developers not to be blindly driven by the novelty of recent developments. If an older method demonstrates superior performance in a particular application or setting, it is better to continue its use. For example, in early tests of updates to the OLCPT, we explored the viability of using BERT to generate embeddings, rather than GPT models. Interestingly, these models severely underperformed relative to expectation. Convergent correlations using BERT-based embeddings were between 0.01 and 0.1. This was likely due to a particular constraint of the BERT model associated with its computational demands and the way that it processes text. That is, to support its bidirectional attention mechanism and multiple transformer layers, BERT limits the length of input sequences to 512 words or tokens. Ultimately, this was an insufficient amount of text data for the model to accurately capture a construct as complex as personality, even when averaging predicted values from multiple text segments for the same CEO.[9] Generalizing this finding, while both small and large developments can present opportunities for enhancing existing measures, their adoption should be carefully evaluated based on the specific needs and context of the tool in question. This approach ensures that continuous improvements to existing tools are guided by practicality and efficacy, rather than solely by the novelty or recentness of technological advances.

Question 3: How Is the Tool Being Applied?

Besides considering what technological advances may improve an existing tool's performance, it is also important to consider the context in which the tool was developed and its compatibility or adaptability to different contexts. Measurement tools tend to be strongly linked to the source and sample from which they are developed. Thus, they are often most effective when applied to data that closely resemble their original sample. When a source or sample is substantively different from the one used to develop a given tool, additional steps are needed to ensure its validity and effectiveness. Again, this was one of the original motivations to develop the initial version of the OLCPT, given prior tools had been developed on disparate samples unrelated to CEOs and used text from sources that were very different from executive language in earnings calls (i.e., essays written by psychology students, Twitter posts, etc.). Moving forward, scholars can apply OLCPT 2.0 to assess executive personality in their own sets of earnings call transcripts for public US firms. However, we would advise against applying the tool to disparate sources or samples – for example, to predict personality for executives in non-US firms or using language from shareholder letters, social media posts, etc. – without further validating it for that purpose.

With any measurement tool, scholars may also need to conduct post hoc analysis to justify using the tool in new contexts that substantively differ from the context in which it was developed. This may be accomplished by applying the tool to predict the construct of interest in the given context and then validating these predictions through content analysis or by comparing the predictions to validated measures for a subset of the sample. This approach can allow scholars to determine whether the tool remains effective when applied in different contexts. In some cases, however, it may be necessary to redevelop or refine the tool for specific application in the new context, particularly when the new source or sample differs substantially in cultural or linguistic aspects. For example, when dealing with non-English language in NLP applications, it is often insufficient (and potentially inaccurate) to simply translate the text into English and apply a tool developed for English. Instead, scholars should retrain or redevelop the tool for the new language. This process ensures that the tool is attuned to the linguistic and cultural nuances specific to that language, thereby enhancing its accuracy and reliability.

Ultimately, the application of tools like the OLCPT is heavily dependent on the similarity between the training and application samples. While applying these tools to similar samples is generally straightforward and effective, divergences in sample characteristics, especially in cultural or linguistic terms, may necessitate additional validation efforts or even a complete retraining of the tool for optimal performance. This adaptability is key to ensuring any given measurement tool's effectiveness across contexts and datasets.

ADDITIONAL RECOMMENDATIONS FOR COMPUTER-AIDED MEASUREMENT

In this section, we offer some additional recommendations for advancing computer-aided measurement in strategy and management research. These recommendations are based on our knowledge of existing work that has applied novel techniques like AI and ML to improve measurement in our field, and our own experience as researchers and reviewers. We hope these suggestions will inspire and guide future research on measurement issues in the field.

Be Familiar with New Methods and Tools

We recommend that strategy and management scholars make an intentional effort to familiarize themselves with new methods and tools that continue to emerge and evolve in the area of measurement. Such methods and tools can offer researchers new opportunities to measure their constructs and phenomena of interest, as well as to address the challenges and limitations of previous work using older measures. For example, a variety of NLP techniques exist that scholars can use to measure constructs and phenomena from textual data like CEO speeches, annual reports, social media posts, online reviews, etc. As illustrated with the redevelopment of the OLCPT, advances in AI and ML provide a strong basis for continuously improving these techniques. However, to correctly apply these techniques and truly improve our understating of the phenomena we examine, scholars must have at least a baseline understanding of how they function and their strengths and weaknesses. Otherwise, we risk adopting novel approaches at the expense of true scientific development and understanding.

Fortunately, the field has established infrastructure to facilitate learning about new measurement techniques. These include methods-specific publications like the present book and similarly oriented journals, professional development workshops at annual strategy and management conferences, and other programs from special interest groups and consortia, such as the research methods communities within the Academy of Management and Strategic Management Society, as well as the Consortium for the Advancement of Research Methods. Whereas a good number of scholars take frequent advantage of these opportunities, our experience is that too many of our colleagues simply do not. As a consequence, we often see outdated methods applied in papers submitted to journals where we serve as reviewers, and we have also seen new methods applied in inappropriate ways.

Of course, we acknowledge it is unrealistic to expect all researchers to keep up to date on all methods and tools that are being applied across strategy and management research. But at a minimum, we should each do our best to become familiar with methods that are relevant to our conceptual domains of expertise. For example, methods that would be most applicable in the strategic leadership domain may differ somewhat from those that would apply in other areas, such as the networks literature, the competitive dynamics literature, etc. As new techniques are applied in these different domains, scholars studying those areas should be familiar with them. Moreover, when applying a new method or tool, scholars should ensure they have carefully reviewed supporting material and that they understand how to properly apply it to their data. By familiarizing ourselves with new methods and tools, we as researchers can expand our methodological toolboxes and enhance our measurement capabilities and competencies. An important note here is that we believe this process should start at the doctoral student stage. Our hope is that more doctoral programs would highlight cutting edge research methods and tools in their seminars and move beyond a general overview of traditional methodologies.

Avoid Overhyping AI and ML Techniques

As we continue to apply novel methods in our field, we also caution scholars against overhyping AI and ML techniques as a panacea or a magic bullet for measurement-related challenges. These techniques are powerful and promising as a way to improve measurement in our field; however, they are not flawless or infallible. They have their own assumptions, limitations, and challenges which scholars need to consider when deciding when and how to apply them. Again, a primary constraint relates to their source and sample specificity, which may limit their applicability or require redevelopment when applying them to a new context. Besides that, AI- and ML-based techniques are extremely complex and often have limited transparency, such that their use may sometimes detract from rather than enhance scientific understanding. Hyde et al. (2023, p. 112) summarize this point well in their discussion of data handling in ML-based applications:

> When constructs are simple or relevant indicators are easily identifiable, applying ML is likely unnecessary, and will also have the added risk of reducing transparency. Indeed, many ML algorithms are so complex that it can be challenging to impossible to understand how they make their predictions, even for those who built them (Rudin, 2019). Hence, for some constructs, the improved accuracy in measurement obtained by applying ML may not justify the decreased transparency.

In addition, as AI and ML techniques continue to evolve, strategy and management scholars should be aware of the ethical issues they may pose. For instance, other fields have begun to explore issues with AI related to privacy and its potential susceptibility to bias that can promulgate inequity and discrimination (Johnson, 2019; Lo Piano, 2020; Zhang et al., 2021). We believe similar investigations that are specific to strategy and management will be necessary to promote the responsible use of these technologies in the future. In any case, scholars should not use AI and ML techniques uncritically or indiscriminately. Applying them appropriately requires informed human judgment. By avoiding overhyping AI and ML, we can maintain a balanced and realistic approach to measurement and avoid potential risks associated with these techniques.

Use Complementary Methods

To further enhance scientific understanding, we also suggest that scholars use complementary approaches to measure their constructs and phenomena of interest, rather than rely on any single or dominant approach. As a field, we should encourage the use of qualitative and quantitative approaches, subjective and objective measures, direct and indirect measures, formative and reflective measures, and static and dynamic measures, depending on the nature and purpose of the research. Applying complementary approaches can improve scientific understanding in strategy and management by allowing us to better capture the complexity and diversity of the phenomena we examine, reducing the potential deleterious effects of measurement error and bias on interpretation, and increasing the validity and reliability of our collective findings.

Referring again to the current exercise as an example, we note that the existence of large-scale language-based measures like the OLCPT does not preclude the usefulness of studies based on alternative methods like videometric or historiometric analysis (Benischke et al., 2019; Gupta et al., 2018; Hill et al., 2019). Not only did these other methods provide the basis for the tool, but they also represent distinct measures whose continued use can help scholars to triangulate, and cross-validate research findings related to executive personality. Also, while strategy research in particular tends to rely heavily on quantitative methods, supplementing this work with qualitative methods like structured interviews, or applying mixed-methodological approaches can enrich our understanding of how organizations function and the mechanisms underlying the relationships we examine (e.g., Boivie et al., 2021; Mannor et al., 2016; Wong et al., 2011). Overall, by using complementary approaches, we can improve the quality and credibility of our research and address potential limitations associated with any given measurement technique.

Be Realistic and Reasonable in the Review Process

We also call for editors and reviewers to be realistic and reasonable about what they ask of authors in the revision process related to measurement. Certainly, editors and reviewers play a critical role in ensuring the quality and rigor of the research published in our field, and they have the right and responsibility to request additional analyses, tests, or validation from authors, particularly when applying existing tools in new or different contexts. Again, as we have served in these roles, we have seen some authors use outdated measures or apply new methods in inappropriate ways. Challenging authors to improve their methods in these cases is not just reasonable but necessary for good science.

At the same time, editors and reviewers need to recognize that the publication burden is already high, and that it is unfair and unrealistic to ask each set of authors to independently validate and revalidate a tool when it has demonstrated acceptable levels of validity and reliability. As editors and reviewers provide feedback regarding measurement, it is important that they consider the costs and benefits of the requests they make of authors, and that they recognize when a new method or tool has already been validated for application in a given context. Here again, it can help for individuals acting in these roles to familiarize themselves with advancing techniques and their development, and to balance their benefits with any inherent limitations. We should not allow the pursuit of perfection to lead to unrealistic standards that create unnecessary barriers to publication without creating value for the field. By following these guidelines, editors and reviewers can encourage more constructive and collaborative relationships with authors during the review process and can facilitate true scientific progress in strategy and management.

Recognize Measurement as a Central Aspect of Organizational Research

Finally, we encourage scholars, editors, and reviewers to recognize that improving measurement does more than just enhance methodological rigor in our field, but that it can also directly contribute to our understanding of organizational phenomena. Improving measurement can be invaluable in helping researchers to define, operationalize, and test their constructs and theories of interest (e.g., Eklund & Mannor, 2021; Gamache et al., 2015; Hyde et al., 2024). It can also allow scholars to challenge and extend existing knowledge (e.g., Harrison et al., 2023; Wilcox-King & Zeithaml, 2003) and to discover new relationships that otherwise would have remained hidden (e.g., Choudhury et al., 2021). Thus, we should not view measurement as a secondary or peripheral aspect of our research, but as a primary and central one.

Along these lines, some of the top journals in our field have recently recognized advances in research methods as a valid criterion for accepting a paper. For instance, in expanding the types of manuscripts considered for publication in the *Academy of Management Journal* to include methods articles, Gruber and Bliese (2024, p. 1) stated, "advances in methods provide opportunities to expand the theoretical scope of management research by offering new ways to develop and test foundational propositions upon which our theories are based." Over the past few years, the *Strategic Management Journal* has also made adjustments to its editorial policies that recognize measure development and database development as contributions to knowledge worthy of publication. We applaud these editorial decisions and encourage editors and reviewers in our field to be open to such methodological advances as meaningful contributions to the field. Doing so can increase incentives for rigorously developed measurement papers, promoting continuous improvement in measurement to support more robust theory.

NOTES

1. The tool went through five distinct iterations using different ML techniques before being made available online. Hence, the initial public release was version 1.5.

2. Other ML algorithms include Decision Trees, Random Forest, Support Vector Machines, Neural Networks, KNN, and Naive Bayes, among many others. For useful descriptions of several of these algorithms, see Choudhury et al. (2021) and Hyde et al. (2023).

3. LLMs as we know them today did not begin to emerge until around 2018, following the development of the transformer architecture (Vaswani et al., 2017), which we will describe below. However, contemporary LLMs largely built on earlier techniques, including the Word2Vec model that provided the basis for OLCPT 1.5. Other important advancements in this area included Doc2Vec in 2014, skip-thought vectors in 2015, and fast-text in 2016. While these models did not reach the extreme scale of later models like OpenAi's GPT-3, they played a crucial role in advancing understanding of pretraining and transfer learning in NLP. For more information about the evolution of LLMs, and ChatGPT in particular, see articles by Arsanjani (2023) and Marr (2023).

4. We acknowledge that other companies have also launched APIs based on their own LLMs, such as Anthropic's Claude, Google's Bard, and Meta's Llama2. For the purposes of this chapter, we focus on OpenAI's GPT because it was the primary originator of the technology and because we use OpenAI's API to redevelop the OLCPT in the following section.

5. We are extremely grateful to each of these coauthor teams for sharing their data and allowing us to use them as a basis for the expanded training sample.

6. One distinction is that the historiometric data from Benischke et al. (2019) were based on broad dossiers of CEOs, which included videos, but also included executive biographies, press releases, and other materials. More information on the data and method used for the historiometric scores is provided in the original paper.

7. These included Linear Models (Linear Regression, Lasso Regression, Ridge Regression, etc.), Tree-based Models (Decision Trees, Random Forest, Gradient Boosting Machines, XGBoosting, etc.), Support Vector Machines, KNN, and Naive Bayes (Gaussian Naive Bayes, Bernoulli Naive Bayes, etc.).

8. Values of K are often in the range of 1–20. Higher values of K tend to result in smoother decision boundaries, leading to simpler models. But they may oversimplify the model and lead to bias or underfitting, especially in smaller samples or when the underlying patterns in the data are complex, as we would expect in the case of assessing personality based on language. Conversely, the main risk of smaller K values is that they may lead to overfitting. However, they are generally more flexible and sensitive to local patterns in the data, meaning they can adapt well to noise and small-scale variations in the dataset. They also require less computational resources during the training process. In our case, we used the default value of $K = 5$ to simplify the training process, as we felt it balanced these tradeoffs of fit with our relatively small and complex dataset. We note that future updates to the tool may include additional experimentation with this parameter. So, users should refer to the online documentation for updates to this and other parameters.

9. As previously suggested, this result was consistent with patterns for OLCPT 1.5, which required a minimum of about 1,000 tokens (words) to generate accurate and reliable scores. This is also why we aggregated CEO texts at an annual level before training models for each trait – to ensure a sufficient amount of text for accurate and reliable predictions.

REFERENCES

Aabo, T., Hanousek Jr, J., Pantzalis, C., & Park, J. C. (2023). CEO personality traits and corporate value implication of acquisitions. *Journal of Empirical Finance*, *73*, 86–106.

Aabo, T., Hansen, J. B., & Petersen, S. M. (2023). Love thy neighbor: CEO extraversion and corporate acquisitions. *Finance Research Letters*, *55*, 103908.

Andrei, A. G., Benischke, M. H., & Martin, G. P. (2024). Behavioral agency and the efficacy of analysts as external monitors: Examining the moderating role of CEO personality. *Strategic Management Journal*, *45*(1), 113–143.

Arsanjani, A. (2023). The evolution of generative AI. *The Medium*. https://dr-arsanjani.medium.com/the-evolution-of-generative-ai-38680ffd425. Accessed on March 4, 2024.

Benischke, M. H., Martin, G. P., & Glaser, L. (2019). CEO equity risk bearing and strategic risk taking: The moderating effect of CEO personality. *Strategic Management Journal*, *40*(1), 153–177.

Boivie, S., Withers, M. C., Graffin, S. D., & Corley, K. G. (2021). Corporate directors' implicit theories of the roles and duties of boards. *Strategic Management Journal*, *42*(9), 1662–1695.

Carpenter, M. A., Geletkanycz, M. A., & Sanders, W. G. (2004). Upper echelons research revisited: Antecedents, elements, and consequences of top management team composition. *Journal of Management*, *30*(6), 749–778.

Carvalho, D. V., Pereira, E. M., & Cardoso, J. S. (2019). Machine learning interpretability: A survey on methods and metrics. *Electronics*, *8*(8), 832.

Chen, T., & Guestrin, C. (2016). XGBoost: A scalable tree boosting system. In *Proceedings of the 22nd ACM SIGKDD international conference on knowledge discovery and data mining* (pp. 785–794). Association for Computing Machinery.

Choi, J., Menon, A., & Tabakovic, H. (2021). Using machine learning to revisit the diversification–performance relationship. *Strategic Management Journal*, *42*(9), 1632–1661.

Choudhury, P., Allen, R. T., & Endres, M. G. (2021). Machine learning for pattern discovery in management research. *Strategic Management Journal*, *42*(1), 30–57.

Colbert, A. E., Barrick, M. R., & Bradley, B. H. (2014). Personality and leadership composition in top management teams: Implications for organizational effectiveness. *Personnel Psychology*, *67*(2), 351–387.

Connelly, B. S., & Ones, D. S. (2010). An other perspective on personality: Meta-analytic integration of observers' accuracy and predictive validity. *Psychological Bulletin*, *136*(6), 1092.

Dale, R. (2021). GPT-3: What's it good for?. *Natural Language Engineering*, *27*(1), 113–118.

Deng, F., Huang, J., Yuan, X., Cheng, C., & Zhang, L. (2021). Performance and efficiency of machine learning algorithms for analyzing rectangular biomedical data. *Laboratory Investigation*, *101*(4), 430–441.

Devlin, J., Chang, M.-W., Lee, K., & Toutanova, K. (2018). BERT: Pre-training of deep bidirectional transformers for language understanding. *arXiv preprint arXiv:1810.04805*.

Eklund, J. C., & Mannor, M. J. (2021). Keep your eye on the ball or on the field? Exploring the performance implications of executive strategic attention. *Academy of Management Journal*, *64*(6), 1685–1713.

Floridi, L., & Chiriatti, M. (2020). GPT-3: Its nature, scope, limits, and consequences. *Minds and Machines*, *30*, 681–694.

Funder, D. C. (1980). On seeing ourselves as others see us: Self-other agreement and discrepancy in personality ratings 1. *Journal of Personality*, *48*(4), 473–493.

Gamache, D. L., McNamara, G., Mannor, M. J., & Johnson, R. E. (2015). Motivated to acquire? The impact of CEO regulatory focus on firm acquisitions. *Academy of Management Journal*, *58*(4), 1261–1282.

Gilpin, L. H., Bau, D., Yuan, B. Z., Bajwa, A., Specter, M., & Kagal, L. (2018). Explaining explanations: An overview of interpretability of machine learning. In *Proceedings of the 2018 IEEE 5th international conference on data science and advanced analytics (DSAA)* (pp. 80–89). IEEE.

Goldberg, L. R. (2000). *International personality item pool*. https://ipip.ori.org/

Gruber, M., & Bliese, P. (2024). Expanding AMJ's manuscript portfolio: Research methods articles designed to advance theory and span boundaries. *Academy of Management Journal*, *67*(1), 1–4.

Gupta, A., Nadkarni, S., & Mariam, M. (2018). Dispositional sources of managerial discretion: CEO ideology, CEO personality, and firm strategies. *Administrative Science Quarterly*, *64*(4), 855–893.

Harrison, J. S., Josefy, M., Kalm, M., & Krause, R. (2023). Using supervised machine learning to scale human-coded data: An illustration in the board leadership context. *Strategic Management Journal*, *44*(7), 1780–1802.

Harrison, J. S., & Malhotra, S. (2023). Complementarity in the CEO-CFO interface: The joint influence of CEO and CFO personality and structural power on firm financial leverage. *The Leadership Quarterly*, 101711.

Harrison, J. S., Thurgood, G. R., Boivie, S., & Pfarrer, M. D. (2019). Measuring CEO personality: Developing, validating, and testing a linguistic tool. *Strategic Management Journal*, *40*(8), 1316–1330.

Harrison, J. S., Thurgood, G. R., Boivie, S., & Pfarrer, M. D. (2020). Perception is reality: How CEOs' observed personality influences market perceptions of firm risk and shareholder returns. *Academy of Management Journal*, *63*(4), 1166–1195.

Hashimoto, M., Terai, M., Maeda, T., & Minami, K. (2015). Extracting facts from performance tuning history of scientific applications for predicting effective optimization patterns. In *Proceedings of the 2015 IEEE/ACM 12th working conference on mining software repositories* (pp. 13–23). IEEE.

Herrmann, P., & Nadkarni, S. (2014). Managing strategic change: The duality of CEO personality. *Strategic Management Journal*, *35*(9), 1318–1342.

Hill, A. D., Petrenko, O. V., Ridge, J. W., & Aime, F. (2019). Videometric measurement of individual characteristics in difficult to access subject pools: Demonstrating with CEOs. In B. K. Boyd, T. R. Crook, J. K. Le, & A. D. Smith (Eds.), *Research methodology in strategy and management* (pp. 39–61). Emerald Publishing Limited.

Hyde, S. J., Bachura, E., Bundy, J., Gretz, R. T., & Sanders, W. G. (2024). The tangled webs we weave: Examining the effects of CEO deception on analyst recommendations. *Strategic Management Journal*, *45*(1), 66–112.

Hyde, S. J., Bachura, E., & Harrison, J. S. (2023). Garbage in, garbage out: A theory-driven approach to improve data handling in supervised machine learning. In A. D. Hill, A. F. McKenny, P. O'Kane, & S. Paroutis (Eds.), *Research methodology in strategy and management* (pp. 101–132). Emerald Publishing Limited.

Johnson, S. L. (2019). AI, machine learning, and ethics in health care. *Journal of Legal Medicine*, *39*(4), 427–441.

Kelvin, W. T. B. (1883). Electrical units of measurement. In *Popular lectures and addresses* (pp. 73–136). Macmillan and Company.

Letzring, T. D., Block, J., & Funder, D. C. (2005). Ego-control and ego-resiliency: Generalization of self-report scales based on personality descriptions from acquaintances, clinicians, and the self. *Journal of Research in Personality*, *39*(4), 395–422.

Li, H., Cai, R., Liu, N., Lin, X., & Wang, Y. (2018). Deep reinforcement learning: Algorithm, applications, and ultra-low-power implementation. *Nano Communication Networks*, *16*, 81–90.

Lo Piano, S. (2020). Ethical principles in machine learning and artificial intelligence: Cases from the field and possible ways forward. *Humanities and Social Sciences Communications*, *7*(1), 1–7.

Mairesse, F., Walker, M. A., Mehl, M. R., & Moore, R. K. (2007). Using linguistic cues for the automatic recognition of personality in conversation and text. *Journal of Artificial Intelligence Research*, *30*(1), 457–500.

Mannor, M. J., Wowak, A. J., Bartkus, V. O., & Gomez-Mejia, L. R. (2016). Heavy lies the crown? How job anxiety affects top executive decision making in gain and loss contexts. *Strategic Management Journal*, *37*(9), 1968–1989.

Marr, B. (2023). *A short history of ChatGPT: How we got to where we are today*. Forbes. https://www.forbes.com/sites/bernardmarr/2023/05/19/a-short-history-of-chatgpt-how-we-got-to-where-we-are-today/?sh=699d6ae8674f. Accessed on November 30, 2023.

Mikolov, T., Sutskever, I., Chen, K., Corrado, G., & Dean, J. (2013). Distributed representations of words and phrases and their compositionality. In *Proceedings of the conference on neural information processing systems* (pp. 3111–3119). Curran Associates Inc.

Miric, M., Jia, N., & Huang, K. G. (2023). Using supervised machine learning for large-scale classification in management research: The case for identifying artificial intelligence patents. *Strategic Management Journal*, *44*(2), 491–519.

Nadkarni, S., & Herrmann, P. (2010). CEO personality, strategic flexibility, and firm performance: The case of the Indian business process outsourcing industry. *Academy of Management Journal*, *53*(5), 1050–1073.

Nie, X., Yu, M., Zhai, Y., & Lin, H. (2022). Explorative and exploitative innovation: A perspective on CEO humility, narcissism, and market dynamism. *Journal of Business Research, 147*, 71–81.

Park, G., Schwartz, H. A., Eichstaedt, J. C., Kern, M. L., Kosinski, M., Stillwell, D. J., Ungar, L. H., & Seligman, M. E. P. (2015). Automatic personality assessment through social media language. *Journal of Personality and Social Psychology, 108*(6), 934–952.

Petrenko, O. V., Aime, F., Recendes, T., & Chandler, J. A. (2019). The case for humble expectations: CEO humility and market performance. *Strategic Management Journal, 40*(12), 1938–1964.

Petrenko, O. V., Aime, F., Ridge, J., & Hill, A. (2016). Corporate social responsibility or CEO narcissism? CSR motivations and organizational performance. *Strategic Management Journal, 37*(2), 262–279.

Radford, A., Narasimhan, K., Salimans, T., & Sutskever, I. (2018). *Improving language understanding by generative pre-training.* https://cdn.openai.com/research-covers/language-unsupervised/language_understanding_paper.pdf

Raffel, C., Shazeer, N., Roberts, A., Lee, K., Narang, S., Matena, M., Zhou, Y., Li, W., & Liu, P. J. (2020). Exploring the limits of transfer learning with a unified text-to-text transformer. *Journal of Machine Learning Research, 21*(1), 5485–5551.

Refaeilzadeh, P., Tang, L., & Liu, H. (2009). Cross-validation. In L. Liu & M. T. ÖZsu (Eds.), *Encyclopedia of database systems* (pp. 532–538). Springer US.

Rudin, C. (2019). Stop explaining black box machine learning models for high stakes decisions and use interpretable models instead. *Nature Machine Intelligence, 1*(5), 206–215.

Tang, Y., Mack, D. Z., & Chen, G. L. (2018). The differential effects of CEO narcissism and hubris on corporate social responsibility. *Strategic Management Journal, 39*(5), 1370–1387.

Tay, Y., Dehghani, M., Abnar, S., Shen, Y., Bahri, D., Pham, P., Rao, J., Yang, L., Ruder, S., & Metzler, D. (2020). Long range arena: A benchmark for efficient transformers. *arXiv preprint arXiv:2011.04006.*

Vaswani, A., Shazeer, N., Parmar, N., Uszkoreit, J., Jones, L., Gomez, A. N., Kaiser, Ł., & Polosukhin, I. (2017). Attention is all you need. *Advances in Neural Information Processing Systems, 30.*

Wilcox-King, A., & Zeithaml, C. P. (2003). Measuring organizational knowledge: A conceptual and methodological framework. *Strategic Management Journal, 24*(8), 763–772.

Wong, E. M., Ormiston, M. E., & Tetlock, P. E. (2011). The effects of top management team integrative complexity and decentralized decision making on corporate social performance. *Academy of Management Journal, 54*(6), 1207–1228.

Yang, M., Adomavicius, G., Burtch, G., & Ren, Y. (2018). Mind the gap: Accounting for measurement error and misclassification in variables generated via data mining. *Information Systems Research, 29*(1), 4–24.

Zhang, B., Anderljung, M., Kahn, L., Dreksler, N., Horowitz, M. C., & Dafoe, A. (2021). Ethics and governance of artificial intelligence: Evidence from a survey of machine learning researchers. *Journal of Artificial Intelligence Research, 71*, 591–666.

Zhang, H., Ou, A. Y., Tsui, A. S., & Wang, H. (2017). CEO humility, narcissism and firm innovation: A paradox perspective on CEO traits. *The Leadership Quarterly, 28*(5), 585–604.

Zhu, D., & Chen, G. (2015). CEO narcissism and the impact of interlocks on corporate strategy. *Administrative Science Quarterly, 60*(1), 31–65.

www.ingramcontent.com/pod-product-compliance
Lightning Source LLC
Jackson TN
JSHW011918131224
75386JS00004B/267